The Complete Psalms

The Complete Psalms

THE BOOK OF PRAYER SONGS IN A NEW TRANSLATION

Pamela Greenberg

Foreword by Susannah Heschel

BLOOMSBURY

NEW YORK • BERLIN • LONDON

Published by Bloomsbury USA, New York

All papers used by Bloomsbury USA are natural, recyclable products made from wood grown in well-managed forests. The manufacturing processes conform to the environmental regulations of the country of origin.

LIBRARY OF CONGRESS CATALOGING-IN-PUBLICATION DATA

Bible. O.T. Psalms. English. Greenberg. 2010.
The complete Psalms : the book of prayer songs in a new translation / [translated by] Pamela Greenberg. — 1st U.S. ed.
p. cm.
Includes bibliographical references and index.
ISBN 978-1-60819-120-8 (alk. paper)
I. Greenberg, Pamela.   II. Title.
BS1424G74 2010
223'.205209—dc22
2009044554

ISBN 9781608191208

First U.S. Edition 2010

1 3 5 7 9 10 8 6 4 2

Typeset by Westchester Book Group
Printed in the United States of America by Worldcolor Fairfield

Contents

Foreword

As Pamela Greenberg writes in her introduction to this extraordinary new translation of the psalms, these are poems written not to formulate religious doctrine, but to give voice to religious emotion—all emotion, from anguish to exaltation, loneliness to thanksgiving, yearning to rage. Where our hearts go, the psalms sing with us.

Hebrew poets wrote the psalms, and their translator must be both a scholar of Hebrew and a poet herself, as is Pamela Greenberg. Her sensitivity to the nuances of the text and her commitment to creating a translation without obstacles, using inclusive language and rendering verses as questions rather than declarations, is a great gift to her readers. Her dedication is to the text but also to those thirsty for the psalms' voices. Greenberg explains: "The psalms have touched people because they reflect the lived experience of religion, not neat theological doctrine." They inspire rather than instruct, and they give voice to the deepest levels of our emotions: "We find within these verses the human search for God in all its mire and mud of complexity . . . a person yearning for revelation."

The psalms appeal to all people, regardless of religious commitments, because they strive to give voice to the human soul. Elusive and often unknowable, our souls and their passions inspire our lives and quest for religious meaning. Not under the discipline of particular theological doctrine, the psalms are free to express the religiosity that gives rise to a wide range of religious commitments, giving them a universal relevance. People of all faiths partake of their invigorating emotional music.

Jewish life receives its flavor from the psalms. We enter, celebrate, and exit our lives in psalms. Birth, death, holidays and fast days, events of joy and sorrow are all expressed through chanting psalms. In Jewish tradition, when a child is being born, mothers and fathers recite psalms. My own mother was given general anesthesia against her will when giving birth to me, but my father spent the night pacing the floor in the hospital waiting room, trying to calm himself by chanting psalms. As a student in Jerusalem, I went to purchase matza shmurah, the special handmade matza, and watched as a dozen bakers rapidly mixed the special flour with drops of water, rolled out the dough, and quickly placed it, very briefly, in the hot oven, all the while singing psalms. It seemed as though not their hands but their psalms were baking the beautiful, delicate matza.

At times of fear—the illness of a loved one—or despair over death, the psalms are with us, not to offer oleaginous consolation nor to replace our emotions with calming sentiments, but to amplify and even intensify our experience. Just as the psalms sing us into birth, so do they accompany us at death; no deceased body is left alone before burial, but is washed and shrouded while psalms are constantly chanted.

What is so remarkable is the ability of the psalms to elevate us to new levels of awareness: They express in words feelings that are at times inchoate, and they allow us to speak in a voice that might otherwise seem inappropriate for a religious person—rage at our enemies, frustration when they defeat us. Those who despise us are God's enemies, the psalmist tells us (Psalm 83), surely a reassuring thought for someone who may feel isolated and deeply fearful in the face of enmity, or who may feel guilty for feelings of anger or resentment. You are not alone, the psalmist explains, and those who despise you, who are an image of God, have become as enemies of God.

Wishes, too, find their voice—if only we could fly away from our fears and horrors, like a dove: "My heart convulses inside; / fear of death has fallen on my soul. Terror and trembling flood through me; / I am overtaken with shudders. Who will give me wings like the dove? / I would fly off and dwell someplace else." (Psalm 55) Such words give voice to our fantasies, and grant us a sense of relief, too, in knowing that our worries are shared by others.

Is prayer for our sake alone? "Barchi nafshi et Adonai," the opening verse of Psalm 103, speaks of our souls giving blessing to God—we pray not for our own sakes alone, but for the sake of God. Even on Yom Kippur, the Bible tells us, two goats are needed—one for Azazel, to atone for our sins, the other for God, to atone for the holy (Leviticus 16:6). Our words of worship as much as our animal sacrifices are offerings that give a "sweet smell," pleasure and strength, to God. The beauty of the psalms as well as their passion are our gifts to God. My father, Rabbi Abraham Joshua Heschel, wrote, "The beginning of prayer is praise. The power of worship is song. To worship is to join the cosmos in praising God."

Prayer is central to religious life, and Jewish prayer is composed not primarily of petition or requests for forgiveness, but of praise of God, as in Psalm 69:31. Prayer is an opportunity for inspiration, a reminder of what we value most highly, and for Jews, prayer begins with psalms. My father viewed prayer as a home for the soul: "To live without prayer is to live without God, to live without a soul . . . To pray is to take notice of the wonder, to regain a sense of the mystery that animates all beings, the divine margin in all attainments. Prayer is our humble answer to the inconceivable surprise of living."

The moments of greatest joy in our lives are fleeting, but when such moments are expressed in the words of psalms they are captured and brought into memory. The psalms express outbursts of joy: "My heart will leap in joy / when you respond to my cry for salvation." (Psalm 13); "I overflow with joy at your presence." (Psalm 16) And God is the "Source of Joy" (Psalm 27, 34, 118), so that moments of our joy are experiences of God. We sing psalms when relieved of torment, when we gather the harvest, when we walk to the chuppah, when we celebrate those we love, when we rejoice in our accomplishments, when we pause and notice the extraordinary miracle of being alive. A psalm every day: is that not what our lives should become?

At the same time, just as prayer comes not simply as a source of comfort and reassurance, the psalms are also intended to disturb our complacency. We pray not only with our hearts and voices, but with our bodies, as the psalmist says, "All my bones will declare: / God, who compares to you, / the one who lifts away the poor / from one more powerful, / the afflicted from hands of the thief?" (Psalm 35) Our bones, our bodies also pray, in acts of kindness, certainly, but also in demonstrations against injustice; in 1965 my father, returning from the civil rights march in Selma, Alabama, said, "I felt my legs were praying."

The passion of the psalms mirrors the passion of the prophets. Both are intended to disrupt our complacency and force us to confront the injustices of our society. From the very first psalm, the message is clear: "The wrongful will not stand in light of justice, / nor the purposeless in gathered testimony of the true of heart." (Psalm 1) We remind ourselves that the very commitment to justice comes from God: "Awaken yourself to my cause / with the justice you commanded of us . . . Bring an end to injuries from the wrongful, / and help sustainers of justice stand upright." (Psalm 7) Indeed, God is known through justice: "Your divinity is known by your justice." (Psalm 9) God is sustained by justice: "Righteousness and justice uphold your holy throne." (Psalm 97) Zion,

Isaiah declares, shall be redeemed by justice, and those who repent, by righteousness. For the psalmist no less than the prophets, justice is the tool of God, the manifestation of God, the means of our redemption, and the redemption of God from human mendacity. With her beautiful new translation of the psalms, Pamela Greenberg helps us move closer to that redemption.

Prof. Susannah Heschel
Dartmouth College

Acknowledgments

I would first of all like to express my deep appreciation to my mother and stepfather, Barbara and Benjamin Zucker, for their great support, emotional, spiritual, and practical. Words cannot say enough. My father, Frank Greenberg, has been an example to me of someone for whom religion is an essential part of existence, and his relationship with God has undoubtedly influenced my own. My husband, Richard Oxenberg, has also been a source of support and help throughout this process, including devoting more time to child care. I also want to thank my teachers and those I have learned from in less formal ways: Phil Weiss, who helped me find my way into and through the maze of religious life and from whom I learned by both conversation and example; Judith Kates, who has always been a wise support and guide; Art Green, who has taught me much about approaching spirituality with creativity and integrity; Rabbi Victor Reinstein, from whom I have learned about relating to God with the entirety of one's heart and mind; and Joel Rosenberg, whom I learn from in all sorts of ways every time we meet. Members of Congregation B'nai Brith, Nehar Shalom, and the Hebrew College Rabbinical School community have stood as both great examples and friends. Although I cannot mention you each by name, you know who you are. My friend and former teacher Mary Karr has been a great supporter of this project, and her help has been indispensable, especially when it came to publication. Of my agent, Lisa Adams of the Garamond Agency, I cannot say enough. She has been a great help in navigating the world of publishing and has become ultimately, also, a friend. Nancy Miller, my editor, has been incredibly supportive and kind, and has helped me clarify my ideas and say things more gracefully than I would have on my own. Finally, I would like to thank the *Washington Post Book World* for publishing a version of Psalm 8, and Missy Daniels and the PBS Religion and Ethics Web site for publishing versions of Psalms 23, 27, 32, and 90.

B'ezrat Hashem.

Introduction

When I embarked on translating the psalms, it was with an impulse both spiritual and literary. Like many, I turned toward them during a dark time. I had fallen into a depression that was part biological, part circumstantial. The translations were, in effect, my attempt to pray during a period when other kinds of established prayer seemed impossible. My practice was to flip through a version with short synopses until I arrived at one that spoke to me on any given day. I was new to religious life, having landed there through sheer desperation, and found within the psalms a model for talking to God. I had begun to teach myself Hebrew, and found that a dictionary helped reveal aspects of their meaning and beauty that had eluded me in the English renditions with which I was familiar.

The psalms became my companions. The voice of the psalmist crying out for God spoke to me in moments of intense despair. The outbursts of joy upon witnessing divine presence in the natural world equally echoed and evoked my wonder. And finally, the psalms spoke to me as poetry, with their mixture of parallelism and narrative, their intentionality of language and form. I was captivated by the internal dialogue and the complexity of ways that a given psalm revealed an emotion or elaborated a theme, and I had great affinity for the themes themselves. The translation began, then, as a very personal project, a labor of necessity and love.

The psalms are essentially about faith, but not as faith is often imagined. Many of us believe it to be an achieved state, a place on a spiritual map, a glow of unwavering belief in relation to God. But such a conception bears little resemblance to the real experience of religious life, which is always a vector, a way of directing and redirecting oneself toward God in various gradations of intensity and confidence.

The psalms have touched people because they reflect the lived experience of religion, not neat theological doctrine. The psalmist does not embody a religious ideal or Kierkegaard's "man of perfect faith." Instead, we find within these verses the human search for God in all its mire and mud of complexity. Their landscape ranges from rocky crags upon which one stands in flight from persecution, to the shadow of God's wings, to rivers and oceans that threaten to drown one in churning waters of despair. Their diversity gives testimony to the life of a person reaching with full heart and intellect toward God, a person yearning for revelation amidst the spectrum of circumstances that life presents. And within that search appears everything from jubilation to hopelessness to the various emotions in between.

In this, the psalms continue to be wholly relevant to our spiritual quests today. One need not even be overtly religious to be moved by their poetry and their honest confrontation with the suffering of existence. Historically, however, their power has been diminished by an insistence on theological dogma. For many years, their intimate connection with the communal prayer life of both Judaism and Christianity was a stumbling block to translating them honestly. At least until recently, liturgy tended to emphasize visions of spiritual perfection over acknowledgment that religious struggle is a necessary aspect of religious life.

As a result, the overwhelming tendency of translators has been to downplay anger at God and reinterpret the psalms in ways that were doctrinally more palatable. They did this based partly on traditional understandings of the text. Rashi, for instance, the most famous medieval Jewish commentator, demonstrates clear discomfort with the idea of the psalms expressing individual suffering, and tends to read many of the psalms (even ones that clearly resonate with solitary outcry) as representing the communal suffering of Israel. Early Christian commentators, on the other hand, tend to interpret the psalms as prefiguring the second coming of Christ. The King James Version has been accused of upholding the divine right of kings. Every translator has brought a theological and ideological concern to these verses.

Since all translation is part interpretation, bringing one's own ideas to the psalms is inevitable. The difficulty is that allegiance to preconceived ideas of piety has often resulted in a flattening of the richness and subtle poetry of the original. For readers of English, this has been a tragic loss. It is precisely the psalms' refusal to engage in theological piety—their overflowing into wild jubilance or anger or deeply wrenching despair—that allows them to resonate as perennial expressions of the human desire to stand simply and unabashedly before God.

My central motivation in this translation was the impulse of *shiru l'Adonai shir chadash*, the imperative to sing to God a new song. I wanted to render the original in such a way that it might be more useful and alive for liturgical and meditative reflection. In doing so, I wanted to find ways to struggle with the poetry and vibrancy of the original psalms while at the same time wrestling with them as pieces of living liturgy. Because my central aim was to bring the text more fully alive as an act of prayer, I did not limit myself to translating any given word in the same way each time it appears. While consistency of language is useful as a pedagogical drumbeat, awakening a reader to repetitions that might otherwise be lost, poetry was for me a higher imperative.

In some instances, this meant translating identical phrases differently. This is the case, for example, with Psalms 103 and 104, both of which begin with the same Hebrew phrase, *Barchi nafshi et Adonai.* In my rendering of Psalm 103, I translate this as "Be wild, O my soul, for the Source of Wonder." In using that language, I wanted to emphasize the utter exuberance that characterizes the rest of the psalm. In Psalm 104, I translate the same lines as "Stand in wonder, my soul, before the Eternal." In that psalm, it is the quiet wonder at God's everlasting presence that seemed more appropriate to reflect.

I also did not limit myself to a single translation of the various names for God, but rather arrived at translations according to the context. My choices were at times based on etymology. The word *Adonai,* for instance, comes from a root meaning "support for a pole of the tabernacle," and so I sometimes translate it as "My Upholder," rather than the more traditional "My Lord." I have also chosen various expressions for the Tetragrammaton, the name for God that by Jewish tradition is unpronounceable. These include "Holy One," "Eternal," or "Creator," depending on the lines that surround it. My goal was to propel the language and concepts of the psalms beyond familiar meanings and translate them in ways that are more expressive of the concepts they embody.

I also wanted to capture the multilayered texture of the Hebrew root, the fact, for instance, that a given word could hold allusions to both an abstract concept and a physical entity in the same three letter combination. Whenever possible, I opted for the corporeal over the conceptual. For example, in translating Psalm 49 I render the first line as "Listen to this all nations, bend down your ears / all who exist under sharp knife of time." "Sharp knife of time" is a way of expressing the Hebrew *heled,* a word whose root means both "length of life" and "digging." "Sharp knife of time," I felt, encompassed both a sense of mortality and the word's other meaning of digging or carving out. This attempt to illuminate the full texture of Hebrew words led me at times to craft additional lines or phrases in order to flesh out the feeling of the original.

Over time, my relationship to the psalms shifted. My first version attempted to replicate the emotional passion of the psalms, and what emerged was a poetic engagement not afraid to take extensive liberties with the text. Then, perhaps with a fear of how academic readers would react to the work, I went over them with an eye toward the literal. Finally, I opted for what I believe to be a middle ground between strict literality and poetic engagement, with the hopes of awakening for the reader new possibilities for speaking with God.

There were places in the psalms, however, where I translated not literally but according to what seemed to be the underlying intent. Passages such as the ones at the end of Psalm 137, for example, gave me pause. At its most literal this passage proclaims the happiness or praiseworthiness of the one who smashes Babylonian infants upon a rock. Given the political reality of cycles of revenge, let alone the repulsive sentiment of the line itself, I struggled with rendering the line as expressing such praise. In the end, I translated it in keeping with the emotion of the previous line, a longing for persecutors to feel the wrongs they had so carelessly inflicted. Instead of the word "children" I use the words "brightest future," and instead of praising the individual who wreaks revenge, I opt for a reading that acknowledges the universality of suffering.

Likewise, I wrestled with the end of Psalm 95, which in biblical idiom seems to be the voice of God proclaiming that the Israelites in the desert would not enter into a place of rest. This psalm is used in Kabbalat Shabbat, the Jewish Friday night service that welcomes the tranquility of Shabbat and the angels of peace that accompany it. To interpret the psalm as ending on a note of such profound divine alienation never sat right with me, and I always understood it by reading the language somewhat differently. The word that gives the phrase a negative emphasis is also a word that in other contexts means "if." In the translation I rendered the line as I made sense of it when praying—as God's voice overflowing with longing, saying softly, "If only they would come to my place of rest . . ." To my mind this better reflected the feeling of the psalm.

There is a long Jewish tradition of wrestling with texts and creatively interpreting (and reinterpreting) them. In Hebrew, the word for innovative readings of this sort is midrash. The hermeneutics of midrash always takes as its starting point the actual text and looks for new ways to understand words or passages based on the language itself. The writer of midrash might say, for instance, "Don't read this word as 'fear,' but read it as 'see.'" Such an interpretation can be justified by the fact that the words for "fear" (as in "fear of God") and "see" are quite similar in Hebrew and in many conjugations look almost identical. And so, despite this being very much a literal translation, often to the point of interrogating the etymology of the Hebrew root, it is also a midrashic translation in that I have from time to time engaged in creative ways of thinking about the text.

I used this approach as well with passages that seem to emphasize the superiority of Israelites over other people. In my translation, I tend to soften such passages due to a conviction that the psalms stand as religious melodies for all people. I feel confident that I have not departed from the spirit of the psalms nor the words on the page, even when departing from the most literal reading of the text. Always I have been guided by the actual language, the emotional tone of the psalm, and the text that has been received by tradition.

A final example of this approach can be found in Psalm 125. The Hebrew word *Yisrael* (Israel) has been thought by many to signify "one who struggles (or who will struggle) with God." In all instances besides this one, I have translated *Yisrael* as "Israel." Here, however, in the context of this psalm and its association with the physical land of Israel, I translated Israel according to its more spiritual meaning, "those who struggle with God."

Because the psalms have been inextricable from my own prayer life, I have approached them with liturgical concern, questioning how they might be of use in furthering the spiritual journey of others. An example of this sort of struggle can be seen around the word *mitzvot*, traditionally translated as "commandments." The word "commandments" always struck me as too legalistic and authoritarian to express what the word conveys in its best sense, which is a wondrous consciousness of God's presence and blessings, along with a reverent commitment to fulfilling God's will. I have tried to evoke that sense of the word in my rendering, and have done likewise with other words and concepts.

One of the most significant difficulties I encountered in translating had to do with the use of gender in the psalms, both in reference to God and in reference to the anonymous representative of humanity. Hebrew is a gendered language, so everything is masculine or feminine, even a door or a table. Indeed, gender is a function of the language's very structure. Although the psalms' subjects are primarily masculine, I have taken the liberty of occasionally translating the word "he" or "man" in the psalms as either the plural "they" or "she" or "woman." In doing this, I mean to suggest to the reader that the psalms speak equally to either gender. They stand as existential testimony, not particularized experience.

In some instances, however, I thought the masculine pronoun important to retain. For one thing, the "he" of the psalms is often a way for the psalmist to articulate his own predicament (and yes, the overwhelming likelihood is that the psalms were written by a man or men), a dynamic of the psalms I felt it important to retain. For another, avoiding the specificity of gender sometimes made the psalm feel too abstract. Translation is always a flawed art, and a translator is always making choices about competing claims. I made such choices as best as I could.

When it came to God, however, I grew increasingly convinced of the need to translate divinity in a way that was neither masculine nor feminine. This was not an easy choice. Avoiding references to gender creates real difficulties in translation, and the liturgical attempts I had heard often sounded awkward and strained to my ear. But I am keenly aware that reference to God as masculine is a stumbling block for many, not to mention theologically inadequate, and the imperative to be inclusive eventually won out. I found that in order to translate with an ear toward poetry, I needed to be creative. Sometimes I changed the third person to the second person, substituting the word "he" with the word "you"; other times I used one of God's attributes in its place. I did my best to preserve both the poetry and vibrancy of these lines.

Besides passages such as these, the psalms contain many words or phrases in which even the simple meaning is ambiguous. Such passages demand interpretation, which I have unabashedly done. In this, I make no pretense to absolute claim on the truth. I invariably translated in keeping with my overall sense of the psalm, often after consulting other renderings, understandings, and commentaries.

Some readers may be troubled at the psalms' often-expressed desire for revenge. To many of us, convinced of the virtues of tolerance and universalism, such an emotion seems an affront to religious life, not a useful expression of it. And when taken as a theological imperative, this is absolutely the case. But such revenge fantasies stand not as expressions of a pious ideal toward which one should strive but rather as deeply human outbursts of insuppressible frustration. They express the truth of what *is*, not the ideal of how things *ought to be*. They further our religious life in much the same way literature does. By finding the expression of our own frustration mirrored in another, we achieve the mimesis and catharsis Aristotle talks about in his *Poetics* as essential qualities of tragedy. I have struggled with such passages, sometimes rendering them in a way that is more generous in tone, but often leaving them to sit with the reader in all their naked humanity.

Such passages may reflect the truth of our experience, but they are still (and should be) troubling. What they reflect is the act of approaching God honestly—with our anger, our sense of moral outrage, our wish for vindication. They remind us that our theological ideals are not, in fact, our prayer. Our prayer always begins exactly where we are, with our particularities of pain and suffering, the particularity of our outrage. Only in this way does the "enemy" of the psalms becomes understandable and useful.

The "enemy" also has a long tradition of being understood as a personification of one's struggle with suffering, such as that of poverty, addiction, depression, or illness. Mitchell Dahood, in the Anchor Bible translation of the psalms, often identifies the Foe as death, drawing upon Canaanite mythology that depicts the battle between Mot (Death) and Baal, two warring gods. Metaphorical readings such as this are in keeping with the psalms' existential tone. I have sometimes, as in Psalm 23, translated the word "enemy" as "fear," as that seems to me more expressive of the psalm's intention.

In bringing a personal approach, I am no different from any other translator. I have my own sense of what makes these words cry and breathe and shout. The psalms have been at my side both during times of overwhelming gratitude and during stretches when it felt like the dark clouds would never lift. Quite often they gave voice to an emotion that I could not fully articulate myself. Through the ups and downs of existence, they have proved deeply instrumental in preserving my faith and sense of the possibility of relating to God.

In many ways, then, the translation reflects my own struggle with the psalms and experience of them as prayers. My wish is that this struggle be continued by the reader. The psalms have been the most loyal accompaniments to my religious life. I hope that the translation proves useful to others as they undertake the adventure of faith, through its many pathways of joy, sadness, or doubt, and through the challenging landscape of emotional expression and prayer.

A Note About the Text of the Psalms

According to religious tradition, the psalms were written by the biblical David. This claim is complicated by the fact that in their superscriptions many psalms are attributed to others—Asaf, the offspring of Korach, Heman the Ezrachite, and Moses, to name a few. Modern scholars dispute the claim that the historical David authored the psalms and tend to believe that they were written over a period of time ranging from the age of David (1100–900 BCE) until well into the Second Temple Period. Psalm 137, for instance, makes reference to the Babylonian Exile, which makes a claim of Davidic authorship extraordinarily problematic, as the Babylonian Exile did not begin until 586 BCE, well after the life of David. Nevertheless, like all biblical literature, the psalms stand on both a historical plane and a mythological one. I have always been moved by the idea of attributing all the psalms to a single individual because their emotional scope is so wide and because they present such a vast and human spectrum of ways to relate to the divine.

While we know very few things about the details of the Temple service in Jerusalem, one thing we do know is that the psalms were used as liturgy very early on, as early as the First Temple Period. Some psalms, such as the Songs of Uplift (traditionally translated as "Songs of Ascent"), were most likely chanted as a worshipper ascended Zion, the Temple Mount. Others almost certainly were chanted as part of the sacrificial rite, and these were quite possibly accompanied by musical instruments. Some, in fact, make direct reference to instrumentation. Fifty-eight psalms are introduced by the Hebrew word *mizmor*, meaning "melodic ode," and thirteen are introduced by the designation *shir*, meaning "song."

Song and chant have long been a way of lifting up our emotions to the divine. Even today, song or chant constitutes a major part of both Jewish and Christian ritual. The modulations of tone that are possible in song allow for a greater expression of passion and intensity than do words alone. Song is a vehicle of both longing and praise, and by its very nature, the act of singing out our suffering to God transforms it.

Other psalms seem more intimate in tone and origin, and it is probably the case that their usage was more personal, at least early on. When sacrifice was replaced by prayer during the Babylonian Exile (586 BCE), the psalms became a central part of the daily, Shabbat, and holiday liturgy, and some of these psalms were incorporated into the communal prayer ritual. The psalms later came to play a central part in Christian liturgy as well, and make up the central part of the Liturgy of Hours, a set of daily prayers in the Catholic tradition. In Protestantism, too, the psalms figure prominently in the liturgy, and have often been set to music as hymns.

The superscriptions, which appear in many but not all of the psalms, are universally believed to be a later addition, and some of the characters mentioned in them are now unknown. It is important to mention that Korach, one of the people who can be positively identified, is portrayed in the Bible as rebelling against Moses, and indirectly against God. To attribute psalms to his offspring is to indirectly affirm the possibility of transformation and atonement.

The psalms also make reference to biblical stories, and I include some of these references in the notes (available online at www.thecompletepsalms.com). Some of the characters, such as

Og and Sichon, are notorious enemies of the people of Israel as they wandered the desert. Other names stand for an entire people, as in the case of Cham, one of Noah's sons. In the Bible, Cham is cursed for having witnessed his father's nakedness, and in the psalms Cham seems to stand for the land of Egypt, the place where the descendants of the biblical Cham ultimately settled. It is not so important to know the identity or context of all the characters who appear in the psalms, as the contents of the psalms stand on their own. It is important to note that some of the people mentioned are archetypal enemies of Israel, such as Og, king of Bashan, and Sichon, king of the Emorites. Both of these are seen as unjustly attacking Israel as it wandered in the wilderness.

A few words in the psalms deserve special mention, as they appear in forms transliterated from Hebrew. One word is "Selah," the meaning of which is somewhat uncertain, but which seems to have the effect of a musical exclamation mark, a sign that what preceded it should receive a certain amount of emphasis. It is more or less untranslatable, so I have let it stand.

Another word is "Halleluyah," a phrase that literally means "praise God." The root *hallel* also means "to shine," and so I have sometimes translated this as "shine your praises on God." In other psalms, I include the word "Halleluyah" in addition to the translation, as it has become so resonant and expressive of passionate praise.

Beyond this, it is important to emphasize that the language of the psalms often comprises unorthodox or ambiguous Hebrew, along with loan words from neighboring dialects. Part of the reason that translations of the psalms differ so widely is because one is compelled to interpret them as one goes along.

Psalm 1

Blessed are those who walked
not influenced by the guilty,

who in the path without purpose did not linger;
in the dwellings of scorners did not long dwell.

They are consumed with the teaching of God
and meditate on divine wisdom both day and night.

They will be like a tree transplanted along a breach in
    the river
that yields fruit at its appointed season

and whose leaves never cease to produce;
all their labor streams forth to fruition.

Not so with those who act wrongly.
They are like chaff carried by changes in wind.

The wrongful will not stand in the light of justice,
nor the purposeless in gathered testimony of the true
    of heart.

Because God attends to the road of the righteous
and the road of the wrongful is covered with weeds.

Psalm 2

Why do crowds rush around restless?
And why do nations contemplate empty goals?

Kings of the earth stand brazenly,
while princes conspire in secret,
against God and against the anointed.

They say:
"Let us break the ropes of their oppression!
Let us throw off the thick weave of heavenly rule!"

The one enthroned in the sky will make light of them,
shrugging at their fearless pride.

Then with words of righteous anger,
God's heavenly disapproval will fill them with dread:

I have anointed my king on Zion,
mountain where my holiness dwells.

I am the one who creates eternal law.

God said to me, *You are my child.*
I give birth to you each day.

Come to me with your perplexities
and I will make people your inheritance;
your possessions will extend to the ends of the earth.

If you break them with a staff of iron,
they will shatter like a vessel of clay.

And now, kings of all countries, awake!
Judges of the earth, discipline yourselves.

Serve the Eternal with wonder
and rejoice that in the divine presence you quake.

Make purity your only weapon,
lest in the heat of holy anger
the way back to your Redeemer be lost.

Because God's outrage at wrong blazes quickly,
happy are those who take refuge in their Creator's
    will.

Psalm 3

A PSALM OF DAVID,
WHEN HE FLED BEFORE ABSALOM, HIS SON.

God, how many are the pursuers that crush against
    me!
Many rise up to wreak my harm.

Many are the ones who say to my soul's flesh:
salvation of God will not come to him—Selah.

But you are the Holy One, a shield that surrounds me
    completely,
source of my glory, the one who raises my head.

When my voice cries out to you,
you answer from your holy mountain—Selah.

I lay down to sleep, but in the morning I awake
because you help me to stand upright.

I will not fear contentious multitudes
who surround me on every side.

Wake up, my Upholder, bring me salvation, my God!

Strike my opposers in the face.
The teeth of the wrongful, shatter them into shards.

God is the source of salvation.
Upon your people is your blessing—Selah.

Psalm 4

>─┼◆>─○─<◆┼─<

FOR THE CONDUCTOR OF THE ETERNAL SYMPHONY,
UPON THE STRINGED INSTRUMENTS,
A PSALM OF DAVID.

In my calling out to you, let the answer be implied,
God who knows my complaint to be a just one.

In times of anguish, you have widened my way.
Now, with overflowing kindness, pay attention to my
    prayer.

Mortals, why do you put my honor to shame?
You lust after emptiness and quest for deception—
    Selah.

But know that the one who loves the Eternal is singled
    out.
My Upholder will listen
when I call out the Holy Name.

Tremble when you contemplate
all the ways you have missed the mark.

Speak to God in your heart,
when you lie upon your bed
speak to the Holy One with your silence—Selah.

Offer as sacrifice only your righteous acts
and put your trust in the Source of Hope.

Many are the ones who say:
Who will illumine for us the good?

You lift the light of your face above us,
placing gladness in my heart
even when the enemy's grain and wine abound.

With peace and contentment, I lie down and sleep.
Because you, God, are with the lonely,
help me to dwell in trust.

Psalm 5

FOR THE CONDUCTOR OF THE ETERNAL SYMPHONY,
WITH A MELODY LIKE A RIVER,
A SONG OF DAVID.

May you hear the speech of my heart, Holy One,
understand my contemplation before I give it voice.

Listen to my cry for compassion,
My Protector and my God,
because it is to you alone that I pray.

God, hear my voice in the morning,
for each dawn I offer my prayer before you
and wait.

Because you are not a power who desires injustice;
No wrongfulness dwells in your chest.

Those who are boastful cannot stand in your gaze.
You reject all who bring about sorrow.

You cause the speaker of lies to be lost.
From blood and deception, you remain far distant.

But bathed in your abundant kindness,
I will enter your temple,

bowing down in your holy sanctuary,
in utter awe of you.

Light in Darkness, lead me with your righteousness,
because of those who watch for my fall.

Make your path before me straight.
Because there is no truth in their mouths.

Their insides are a chasm of destruction,
their throats an open grave.

Their tongues are slippery.
Do you hold them to account for their guilt?

Let them fall in their scheming.
Because of their many transgressions, push them
    away,
for it is against you they have rebelled.

And let all who take refuge in your presence rejoice.
Let them cry out your praise to the world—

you give them shelter.
Let them exult, all lovers of your name.

Because you, God, bless those who act rightly,
enfolding them with approval like a shield.

Psalm 6

FOR THE CONDUCTOR OF THE ETERNAL SYMPHONY,
ON AN EIGHT-STRINGED INSTRUMENT,
A PSALM OF DAVID.

God, in your anger, do not rebuke me;
in your wrath do not punish me more than I can bear.

Be gentle, my Physician, for I am feeble.
Heal me, for my bones shudder with terror.

My soul multiplies terrors—
and you, God, how long must I wait?

Turn toward me, my Protector;
provide my soul means of escape.
Save me in keeping with your kindness.

For there is no memory of you in death.
In the pit of the underworld who will praise you in
    grateful psalm?

I am worn out by my groans.
Every night, I drench my bed with fevered sweat.

I melt my sickbed with tears of supplication.
My eye is devoured by grief,
grown old from all my wars with suffering.

Turn from me, all implements of sorrow.
God has already heard the sound of my lament.

God has heard my plea; God will take inward my
    prayer.
All my obstructors will be humbled, stricken with
    terror.

My enemies will face themselves and instantly fall to
    their knees.

Psalm 7

>-+-◦-+-<

A PSALM ABOUT GOING ASTRAY, BY DAVID,
THAT HE SANG TO GOD
CONCERNING THE DEEDS OF CUSH,
SON OF YEMINI.

My Foundation, my God, it is in you I have taken
    refuge.
Deliver me from all pursuers;
lift me from all trajectories of harm

lest they ravage my soul's flesh like a lion
gnawing my limbs, leaving no means of relief.

My Foundation, my God, if I have deserved this,
if there is injustice hidden in the palms of my hands,

if I have repaid with ill wishes those who intended
    only good,
if I have withdrawn from those who provoke me
    without cause,

let my enemy chase after my soul's flesh and
    overtake it.
Let him trample my life's blood to the ground;
let my honor from then forward dwell in dust—
    Selah.

Arise, God, in your anger.
Strip away the arrogance of my opposers.

Awaken yourself to my cause
with the justice you commanded of us.

When the tumult of nations surrounds you,
you can return to your heights.

You who hold nations to account,
judge me with favor,
because of my rightness and the innocence I
    represent.

Bring an end to injuries from the wrongful,
and help sustainers of justice stand upright.

For you are righteous;
you search through our hearts and minds.

My shield is the Transcendent,
the Source of Kindness who saves
the straightforward of heart.

You judge with favor the righteous;
you grow outraged every day.

If my enemy refuses to turn back,
my Protector will sharpen the heavenly sword.

The bow is already bent and aimed.
For the unjust, my Guardian
has prepared the weapon of destruction.

The Holy One will use arrows
against those who blaze in pursuit.

Look, my enemy binds himself to bereavement.
He is pregnant with schemes but gives birth only
    to fog.

He shoveled a pit and continued digging:
he fell into his very own trap.

Labor of wrongfulness will come back upon his head.
Upon his brow, his own violence will fall.

I will spill out gratitude to my Source of Hope for
    acting rightly;
I will sing out the name of God, Most High.

Psalm 8

>⊸+⊷–0–⊶+⊸

FOR THE CONDUCTOR OF THE ETERNAL SYMPHONY
UPON THE WINE FESTIVAL LYRE,
A SONG OF DAVID.

God, our Upholder, how vast is your signature
over all the earth.

It reflects your glory in the heavens.

From the mouth of infants and nurslings
you have made a foundation of strength—

to oppose those who oppose you,
to bring the enemy and person of vengeance to a
    halt.

When I behold your name in the heavens,
the craft of your fingers,
the moon and the stars that you fixed immutable,

I think: What is a mortal that you should be mindful
    of him,
offspring of flesh that you should pay her attention?

Yet you have made us only slightly less than God.
You have encompassed us with glory and splendor.

You allow us dominion over the works of your hands;
you placed everything under our feet,

flocks of sheep and herds of cattle, all of them,
every beast of the field.

The bird of the sky and fish of the ocean,
all that traverses the sea.

God, our Upholder,
how vast is your signature
over all the earth.

Psalm 9

FOR THE CONDUCTOR OF THE ETERNAL SYMPHONY,
CONTEMPLATING THE DEATH OF LAVAN,
A PSALM OF DAVID.

I will thank you, God, with the fullness of my heart.
I will tell and repeat all your wonders.

I will rejoice and exult in you,
singing out your name—the greatest praise that exists.

When my enemies turn to attack from behind
they stumble and are lost from before your face.

For you uphold my justice and my cause.
You sit on a throne, sustaining what is right.

You rebuke nations, causing the wrongful to fall into
    ruin.
You erase their name from the testimony of time.

The enemy—their remnants are ravished for eternity;
cities that you have uprooted; their memory is gone.

But you dwell forever in heaven,
steadying your throne for judgment.

You consider all people of the world rightly,
judging nations with clarity of intent.

May you be a lofty refuge for those of crushed spirit,
a place of safety in times of distress.

Those who know your nature will trust you—
you never abandon those who seek you out.

Sing out to God, enthroned in Zion.
Proclaim to nations the holy presence.

The seekers of blood—you remember their carnage,
never ignoring when the humble cry.

Bend toward me, my Help; relent.
See my suffering at the hands of my foes.

Lift me beyond the gates of death,
so I can chant all your praises.

Within the gates of Zion's daughter,
I will rejoice at your salvation.

The people sank in the trap they constructed;
in its net, their legs were tangled in snares.

Your divinity is known by your justice;
in your palms, the wrongful are brought to a halt.

Consider this—Selah—
the wrongful descend to the world of the half-living,
all who have forgotten your name.

But not for eternity are the starving forgotten,
nor is the hope of those who suffer
lost to testimony of time.

Rise up, God, don't allow a mortal to wield wildly
the power for wrong.
Let nations be judged in the light of your face.

Spread, God, your teaching over them
so the people will learn their human frailty—Selah.

Psalm 10

Why, God, do you stand so distant?
You let yourself remain hidden in times of distress.

The unthinking, in arrogance,
flames in pursuit against the afflicted.

Eventually they are caught in the very plans they
    contrived.

Because the unjust
gloat over their soul's least desire,

and the plunderer blesses
while blaspheming against God.

The wrongful with their smug smiles
do not seek you.

Their only slogan is to proclaim,
"God does not exist."

Their ways are well established;
your statutes remain far from their face.

All dangers they breathe away like dust.

They say in their hearts, "Me, I will not falter;
from generation to generation I will come to no harm."

Their mouths are filled with promises—
all of them treachery and deceit.
Under their tongues lurk guile and guilt.

They crouch in ambush amidst courtyards;
from hiding, they strike out against the innocent
to kill them.

Their eyes keep watch for the luckless.
They crouch in secret, like a lion in thicket.

They lie still, waiting to leap upon the weak.
They leap upon the frail, drawing them into their net.

They crush them, bringing them down.
Under their limbs, the weak collapse,
lacking strength to fight.

They say in their hearts, "God has forgotten.
The Holy One no longer cares
and will never bear witness."

Rise up, Source of Strength,
raise up your hand of involvement.
Don't ignore the afflicted.

Why have they scorned God?
They say in their hearts,
"God will not seek me out for punishment."

Look! For you see those who act with cruelty.
To respond is in the power of your hand.

The luckless are ready to leave you.
The orphans—you used to be their help.

Break the muscle of the destructive!
You allegedly seek out evil,
but refuse to bring the wrongdoer to light.

But you, God, your power is eternal;
nations vanish from your earth.

The hope of the afflicted,
you have surely heard it, Source of Justice.

Strengthen their hearts; listen closely with your ears—
to champion the orphan and the poor,

so that wrongfulness will not again grow rampant
to frighten a mortal from the earth.

Psalm 11

FOR THE CONDUCTOR OF THE ETERNAL SYMPHONY,
BY DAVID.

In God I have found refuge.
How can they say to my soul, then,
fly from your mountain like a bird?

For behold, the wrongful bend back their bows.
They aim their arrows on gut strings

to shoot in deep darkness,
to wound those who strive to live justly.

When they assault the foundation of morality,
the righteous—what can they do?

God remains in a holy chamber.
The Eternal remains on a throne in the sky—

with eyes that look down and drink deeply,
with pupils that understand humankind.

God, you may test the righteous.
But the heartless and lover of violence—
you see through their souls.

You rain down snares
on those who act wrongly,

fire and sulfur and raging heat—
that is the portion of their cup.

Because you are righteous,
loving those who act rightly.

You see that their faces
are pointed straight ahead.

Psalm 12

FOR THE CONDUCTOR OF THE ETERNAL SYMPHONY,
ON AN EIGHT-STRINGED INSTRUMENT,
A PSALM OF DAVID.

Help me, God, for kindness exists no more.
The honest have vanished from among humankind.

Each person speaks emptiness to his neighbor.
Their lips are slippery, a language of half-truths.
They speak with double-edged heart.

God, strike the root of all who speak with deception,
the tongue that glorifies the self,

the ones who brag: "Our tongues make us invincible,
our lips are weapons: Who is more godly than us?"

They insulate themselves from the suffering of the
    afflicted,
ignoring the groans of the poor.

"Now I will arise," says God.
"I will place a path of salvation before the righteous;
it will blow toward them like wind."

Each word that God speaks is pure,
silver refined in the earth's crucible,
purified sevenfold.

You, God, keep watch over the righteous.
Protect them from this generation
now and forever.

They will walk exalted among the wrongful,
even when ideals have evaporated
from the rest of humankind.

Psalm 13

FOR THE CONDUCTOR OF THE ETERNAL SYMPHONY,
A PSALM OF DAVID.

Until when, God?
Will you forget me continually?

How long will you hide from me the kindness of your
    face?
How long can I hold back the proof in my chest?

My heart groans by daylight.

How much longer will you raise up enemies
to gloat over my ruin?

Gaze down! Answer me, God, my Protector.

Bring light to my eyes lest I dream the sleep of death,
lest my enemy proclaim, "I have destroyed him."

My oppressor rejoices when I stumble.
But I trust in the constancy of your love.

My heart will leap in joy
when you respond to my cry for salvation.

I will sing out to God
for having rewarded me well.

Psalm 14

▸⭢⬦⭢○⭠⬦⭠◂

FOR THE CONDUCTOR OF THE ETERNAL SYMPHONY,
BY DAVID.

The walking corpse says in his heart,
"There is no God."

They destroy and spoil the holy.
There is no one who labors for good.

God gazed down from heaven upon all humanity
to see whether there existed a person of
    understanding,
one who was searching for truth.

All of them have turned away.
Together, as one, they have grown rancid.

There is no one who labors for good,
not even one.

Do they not know, all inflictors of harm;
those who devour my people
as though devouring bread—

because they do not call upon God,
they will be paralyzed with endless fear.

For the Eternal Judge
is with the generation of the righteous.

You have scorned the counsel of the afflicted,
saying, "Let God be their refuge."

Who can bring salvation to Israel from Zion?

When God returns the people from captivity,
Jacob will exult;
Israel will rise up with joy.

Psalm 15

A PSALM, BY DAVID.

God, who can dwell in your tent?
Who can live on your holy mountain?

The one who walks with integrity,
who acts according to what is right,

who speaks truth from her heart,
and does not let slander tread on her tongue,

who has not acted wrongly to any creature,
does not cast reproach upon any kin,

for whom that which God rejects
is like stolen plunder in her eyes,

the one who reveres
all who hold the Eternal in awe,

who takes an oath about another's wrongdoing
without retracting out of fear,

who does not lend silver at interest,
and a bribe against the innocent will not accept.

The one who does this will never stumble
as long as she lives.

Psalm 16

A SONG LIKE GOLD, BY DAVID.

Watch over me, God, for it is in you I have taken
    refuge.

In the past I said: "You are my Creator,
but you do not look out for my good.

With the holy ones buried in the earth,
and the mighty, in them I have placed all
my hope for protection."

Their sadness multiplies, all who rush after futility,
those who chase after empty gods.

I won't pour out to them blood libations,
won't lift their names in blessing upon my lips.

God is the measure of my portion and my cup.
You uphold my destiny.

Blessings have fallen upon me in pleasant meadows,
wonders and beauty have been my inheritance.

I will praise God, who has given me good counsel.

Even when my fears torment me at night,
I will keep the Eternal always before my eyes.

For when you are at my right arm,
I do not stumble.

My heart leaps up,
the place of my innermost glory rejoices.
Even my flesh rests secure.

For you won't abandon my life to the underworld;
the Holy One will not relinquish the kindhearted
to witness destruction.

Make known to me the pathway of life
until I overflow with joy at your presence,

the lasting contentment that comes from your right
    hand.

Psalm 17

A PRAYER, BY DAVID.

Listen, God, to what is right.

Pay attention to my pain;
open your ears to my cry of prayer—

it does not come from lips that speak idly.

My cause goes out before you,
your eyes pierce through my flesh.

You tested my heart.
You scrutinized it at night.

You smelted me,
but found nothing impure.

Cruel thoughts did not cross my mouth;
our deeds, as I know,
should be in keeping with your will.

I kept myself distant from pathways of the violent.

You supported my steps on your footpaths.
My strides did not stumble underneath.

I called out to you because you answer me, God.

Lean down your ear toward me;
listen to my speaking.

Make your kindnesses distinct
so I can see them.

Save those who seek your refuge
by lifting your right arm.

Guard over me the way an iris keeps watch over an
    eye.
Under the shadow of your wings, give me shelter.

Because the wrongful wreak destruction;
mortal enemies circle all around.

Their gluttony closes in; their mouths speak with
    boastful pride.
Our footsteps—now they surround us.

They turn their eyes to spread over our land.

Those who scheme wrong look like a lion,
greedy to tear off limbs—
like a young lion, crouching in hiding.

Rise up, God, confront them to their face,
humble them to their knees.

Preserve my soul with your sword—
save me from one who intends destruction—

so I will be among those who die by grace of your
    hand, God,
those who perish from old age.

Their portion is life;
their wombs are filled with your treasure.

They are sated with children
and bestow all their goods to their young.

Allow me to behold your face, for I am righteous.
I will be sated with your image every time I awake.

Psalm 18

FOR THE CONDUCTOR OF THE ETERNAL SYMPHONY,
BY A SERVANT OF GOD, BY DAVID,

WHO SPOKE THESE WORDS OF SONG
ON THE DAY THAT GOD PULLED HIM FROM THE PALMS
    OF HIS ENEMIES,
AND FROM THE HAND OF SAUL.

And he said,

I will love you the way a mother loves
her womb's child,
Holy One, my Source of Strength.

You are my cleft in the mountain,
my resting down of weapons,
my deliverer from harm.

You are my Rock:
in your Holy Presence I take shelter.

My shield and my light of salvation,
my high place off from war.

When I shine forth praises to you,
I am lifted from my enemies away.

Cords of death surrounded me,
rivers of my worthlessness and ruin
thrust me into terror.

I was strangled by rope of the underworld.
Snares of death lay waiting wherever I went.

In my constriction, I would call out to you;
to your name I would cry for salvation.

You listened to my voice from your sanctuary.
My pleas for help would come before your ears.

The earth quaked and trembled.
Foothills of the mountains shuddered confused.

They trembled because smoke rose from your nostrils;
a devouring fire raged from your mouth.

Flaming coal fell, burning.
You spread a crack in the heavens and descended,
heavy darkness under your feet.

You mounted an angel and soared.
You flew on breathing wings.

You made darkness your concealment;
a sheltering canopy all around—

dark molten water, clouds of pulverized dust.
From a shining light before you,
black clouds passed overhead, hail and burning coals.

Then you thundered in the sky,
the highest of the high gave forth voice,
hailstorms and burning coals.

You sent forth arrows and scattered them,
a flood of lightning bolts and frenzied them.

The streambeds lit up;
The earth's foundation was stripped bare.

By your rebuke, God, by the wind
that breathed from your nostrils.

You reached down from the heights
and took me;
you drew me from tumultuous waters;

you delivered me from more powerful foes,
from my despisers, for they were stronger.

They confronted me on the day of my ruin,
but you were my staff of support.

You brought me out to broad places.
You drew me from harm, for you desire me.

You repaid me according to my righteousness.
You restored my hands until they were pure as corn.

I have held to your pathways, God;
I have not turned away from my Upholder.

Because your ways of justice stand stark before me,
I will not shrug off your statutes.

I have been honest with you,
guarding myself from twisting away from your will.

And you repay me according to my righteousness,
according to the purity of my hands before your
    eyes.

With the kindhearted you make yourself kind,
with those of simplicity you respond simply.

With the clean of heart, you respond cleanly,
and with the twisted you respond in twists.

For you support those who are humble,
and arrogant eyes you bend down low.

For it is you who light up my candle.
It is you, my God, who makes my darkness shine.

Because with you I can outrun a troop of pursuers,
with your help I can leap over a wall.

The one true God—your path is fulfilling.

Your word is refined and sifted,
a shield of protection to all who take refuge in your
    will.

For who is more divine than the Holy One?
Who is a Rock except our Upholder?

The God who clothes me is a source of strength.
You make my journey's road complete.

The one who strengthens my legs like the rams
and stands me on the highest peaks.

Who teaches my hands to defend themselves,
my arms to hold a bronze bow.

You gave me your shield of salvation;
your right hand held me upright.

Your humility enlarged my heart.
You widened my stride beneath me;
with you my ankles never stumble.

I pursued my enemies and overtook them;
I did not turn until I made them obsolete.

I struck them until they could no longer rise.
They fell beneath my legs.

You girded me with courage for battle,
brought the violent to kneel under my feet,
turned toward me the back of their necks.

My despisers, I annihilated into silence.
They pleaded for help, but there was none to save
      them,
to you, but you gave no response.

I crumbled them like dust in the wind.
I made them vanish like mud in the streets.

You removed me from the people's contentions.
You made me a leader of nations.

People I don't know
now serve me.
Because of what their ears have heard, they listen.

When strangers deceive me, they grow terrified;
they enclose themselves behind walls.

My God is living; my Rock, a source of blessing.

My source of salvation is lifted high,
the God who requites all my wrongs.

You speak to nations in my place,
offering escape from my foes.

Even when people rise up against me,
you lift me away from harm.
From those intending violence, you bring me to safety.

For this I will thank you among the nations, God,
I will sing out praises of your name.

You save your enthroned one over and over,
performing acts of kindness to your anointed,

to David and his seed,
from now until the end of time.

Psalm 19

FOR THE CONDUCTOR OF THE ETERNAL SYMPHONY,
A PSALM OF DAVID.

The sky unfolds story of your presence;
the firmament tells of the work of your hands.

Day after day overflows with speech;
night after night breathes out knowledge.

There is no word or phrase
in which the voice of your creation is not heard.

Throughout all the earth, rope
of their hopefulness goes forth,

and their words reach the end
of the world's long stretch of land.

The sun makes a tent for them
and like a groom rushes forth
from the canopy of marriage.

It springs up like an athlete
ready to run a race.

From the edge of the sky, you bring it;
its sweep continues until the horizon's long stretch of
    land.
Nothing remains untouched by its warmth.

Your teaching is everywhere,
reviving the soul.

Your testimony is faithful,
enlightening those who do not understand.

Your providence can be easily seen,
making the heart leap with joy.

The tasks you ask us to do are revealed clearly,
making the eyes sparkle with light.

Awe of you is pure, lasting forever.
Your decisions are true;
taken together, they prove righteous.

They are more valuable than gold,
more than refined gold in abundance,

better than the sweetest honey,
sweeter than fresh drippings of the hive.

Your servant is brightened in performing them;
keeping them alive brings intrinsic reward.

Unwilling sins, who can glimpse them?
My hidden faults, wash from me their stain.

From purposeful acts of transgression,
hold back your servant's hand.
Don't let them rule over my reason.

Then I will be wholehearted,
cleansed from outright revolt.

May the words of my mouth
and the contemplations of my heart

be in keeping with your will,
God, my Rock and my Redeemer.

Psalm 20

FOR THE CONDUCTOR OF THE ETERNAL SYMPHONY,
A PSALM OF DAVID.

God will answer you on the day of your anguish.
The name of Jacob's Strength
will lift you high above harm.

The Eternal will send you help
from the holiest of places,
and from Zion hold you upright.

The All-Knowing will remember
all your grain offerings,
and consume your burnt offerings with delight—Selah.

The Holy One gives to you
according to the contents of your heart.
All your hopes will be fulfilled.

In the end, we will sing out at your salvation,
raise a flag in the name of our God.

The Source of Hope answers all your questions.

Now I know, God, that you will raise up your
    anointed one,
responding from the holiness of heaven.

With the strength of your right arm,
rescue will surely come.

These with chariot, these with horses,
but we through name of our Upholder
are brought awestruck to remember.

They were bowed to their knees and fell,
but we rose to our feet and will give witness.

You are the source of our salvation,
the Strength who will answer us
on the day we cry out for relief.

Psalm 21

For the Conductor of the Eternal Symphony,
a psalm of David.

God, in your power, the king rejoices.
When he sees your salvation, how intensely he exults!

You have given him the desires of his heart.
And the yearnings of his lips—you have not refused
    them—Selah.

Because you anticipated his needs with blessings of
    goodness.
You placed upon his head a golden crown.

He asked from you only life and you gave him
the length of days under witness of time.

His honor is great because of your saving power.
Glory and splendor—you made him worthy of it.

For you gave him eternal blessings,
the joy of beholding the brightness of your face.

For the king puts all his trust in you.

Because of your kindness,
he does not stumble.

Your hand, God, uncovers all enemies.
Your right hand finds all who despise what is good.
They will feel your presence as a blazing oven.

Let your wrath, God, swallow them whole;
let them be devoured with your fire.

Let their fruit be lost from the earth,
their seed from among the offspring of humankind.

For they reached out in wrongfulness against you.
They contemplated schemes,
but could not bring them to completion.

For you have placed your shoulder against them.
You aim your bowstring at their face.

Raise yourself up, God, in your power.
We will sing out and make melodies
to your unflinching strength.

Psalm 22

FOR THE CONDUCTOR OF THE ETERNAL SYMPHONY,
UPON WITNESSING THE DEER AT DAWN,
A PSALM, BY DAVID.

My God, my God, why have you forsaken me?
You keep yourself distant from my cries,
words that I roar out in pain.

My Protector, I call out by day and you do not answer,
by night and can find no rest.

But you are holy;
you reside in the praises of Israel.

In you our ancestors trusted.
They trusted, and you brought them relief.

To you they cried out, and they were delivered.
They trusted you and came to no shame.

But I am a worm and not a man—
scorned by people, despised by humankind.

All who see me mock me.
Their mouths fall in astonishment;
they shake their heads in contempt.

Whoever turns to God will find relief,
for you will save them, taking pleasure in their faith.

For you are the one who broke me forth from the
    womb,
who taught me trust from my mother's breasts.

Upon you I have been cast since conception.
From my mother's insides you have been my Sustainer.

Don't distance yourself from me, for trouble
   approaches
and there is no one else to bring help.

A stampede of bulls surrounds me.
The violent of Bashan gather all around.

Their mouths foam against me.
A lion tears at my limbs and roars.

Like water I am poured out;
all my bones split apart.

My heart has become like wax,
melting within my organs.

My strength has dried up like a shard of clay.
My tongue cleaves to my jaw.

Into the dust of death you have thrown me like trash.
Wild dogs surround me.

A circle of the wrongful closes in,
like a lion craving my hands and legs.

I can count all my bones.
They gaze at me, staring with greed.

They divide my clothes among themselves,
casting lots upon my garments.

But you are God—don't be distant!
My ram of protection, rush to my help!

Lift my soul from the sword.
From the claws of the dog, keep me intact.

Save me from the lion's mouth
and from the antelope's horns—answer my plea.

I will proclaim your name to my brothers and sisters.
In the midst of an assembly I will shine out your
    praise.

Those who hold you in wonder—give praise.
All offspring of Jacob—give thanks to heavenly glory.

Tremble before the Holy One, all seed of Israel,
for God does not spurn the affliction cries of the poor.

You do not hide from the sorrowful;
when they cry out for salvation, you listen.

My praise for you pours forth in large gatherings.
I will fulfill my vows before all who hold you in awe.

The humble will eat and be satisfied,
they will praise you, all who seek you out—

may their hearts always be hopeful.

Those who live at the earth's ends will remember
and turn back to their Creator.

They will bow down before you, all families of nations.
For to you belongs ultimate allegiance;
it is you who give the people direction.

Let those who eat from the land's bounty
bow down before you in praise.

All who go down to the dust will kneel to you,
along with the one whose life is no longer alive,
the seed of those who serve you.

You will be remembered in every generation.

They will come and tell of your righteousness
to those newly born,
speak forever of the wonders you have done.

Psalm 23

A PSALM OF DAVID.

God is my shepherd; there is nothing I lack.
You lay me down in lush meadows.

You guide me toward tranquil waters,
reviving my soul.

You lead me down paths of righteousness,
for that is your way.

And when I walk though the valley, overshadowed
    by death,
I will fear no harm, for you are with me.

Your rod and staff—they comfort me.
You spread a table before me
in face of my greatest fears.

You drench my head with oil;
my cup overflows the brim.

Surely goodness and kindness
will accompany me all the days of my life

and I will dwell in the house of the Holy
for the length of my days.

Psalm 24

By David, a psalm.

The earth belongs to God and all that fills it,
every continent where people dwell.

For the Creator established its foundations upon the
    oceans
and upon rivers made it firm.

Who can ascend the eternal mountain?
Who can rise to the place where holiness dwells?

The clean of hands and the clear of heart,
those who do not say "By my life"

when they do not mean it,
who do not swear to that which is a lie.

Such ones will carry with them a blessing from God,
a blessing of justice from the God of salvation.

This is the generation of those who seek out your
    wonder,
those among Jacob who quest for your face—Selah.

Lift up your heads, gates of heaven
and the openings of eternity will be lifted.

The Holy One of Glory comes.
Who is this Holy One of Glory?

God, who is strong and valiant,
God, who is unflinching during war.

Lift up your heads, gates of heaven;
lift up the openings of eternity,

The Holy One of Glory comes.
Who is this Holy One of Glory?

Creator of the Heavenly Spheres.
God is the Holy One of Glory—Selah.

Psalm 25

By David.

To you, God, I lift up my soul.
My Help, it is you I have trusted.

Don't let shame overtake me.
Don't let my enemies exult over my ruin.

Do the same for all who put their hope in you.

Let the betrayers fall to shame instead,
those who deceive without cause.

Your roads, God, let me know them.
Your pathways, help me recognize them from the rest.

Lead me down the way of your truth;
teach me its nature.

For you are the God of my salvation.
It is you whose presence I have hoped for all day.

Remember your compassion, Source of Wonder, and
    your kindness,
for they have sustained the world from the beginning
    of time.

The error of my youth and my rebellions,
try to forget them.

Remember me, instead, by the light of your
    kindness—
do it, God, because you are good.

You are gentle and straightforward,
guiding those who stray on the path—

leading the humble to walk in justice,
teaching the willing the holy road.

All your paths are kindness and truth
to those who uphold the covenant
and bear witness to your word.

For the sake of your name, God,
forgive my guilt, for it is overwhelming.

Who reveres you?
You will teach her the path she should choose.

Her soul will sleep content in knowledge of goodness.
And her offspring will inherit the earth.

Your secret is revealed to those who understand your
    wonder,
the covenant understood by those who teach it with
    joy.

My eyes look toward you continually, my Redeemer,
for you release my legs from the snare.

Turn toward me and awaken your compassion,
for I am alone and dejected.

The anguish of my heart widens.
From the constraints of my circumstances,
lead me out.

See my affliction and suffering.
Lift away all my wrongs.

See my enemies, for they multiply.
Those of violence and hatred despise me.

Watch over my soul and bring me to safety.

Don't let me fall to shame
for taking refuge in your will.

Simplicity and clarity will watch over me,
for in you I still put my hope.

God, redeem Israel,
save them from all their confusion and strife.

Psalm 26

Judge me, God,
for I have walked with integrity;

I have trusted your truth
and will never be shaken.

Scrutinize me, God, put me to the test.
Smelt like metal my emotions and mind.

For I hold your kindness before my eyes always
and have walked back and forth in your truth.

I have not dwelt with those who die empty.
Those who conceal their wrongs—
I do not enter their midst.

I have avoided gatherings of the violent.
In the company of the callous, I did not dwell.

I wash my hands clean,
and turn toward your altar, Holy One—

to make my voice of thankfulness heard,
to tell stories of the array of your wonders.

God, I have loved the inside of your temple,
the place where your glory dwells.

Don't associate my soul with the mistaken,
and with the bloodthirsty, my life—

those whose hands pursue selfishness,
whose right arm takes money from bribes.

Because I have walked with integrity,
save me with your compassion.

My foot is planted on level ground.
In gatherings of multitudes I fall to my knees,
in awestruck praise of you.

Psalm 27

By David.

You are my light and my hope;
whom should I fear?

You are the strength of my life;
before whom should I tremble?

When the wrongful approach to devour my flesh,
my oppressors and enemies,
it is they who stumble and fall.

If an encampment pitches tents against me,
my heart will not quiver.

If a war rises up against me,
in you I still trust.

One thing I have asked from you,
one thing I seek,

to dwell in your house
all the days of my life,

to behold your beauty,
to enter your innermost sanctum.

You cover me with the tabernacle of your presence
on days when hardship comes.

You shield me in the concealment of your tent.
Upon a rock, you lift me high from harm.

And now, God, raise my head
above the troubles that surround me.

In your tent, I will make my songs into offerings,
singing forth all my melodies to your name.

Listen, God, to my voice when I call out.
With compassion, answer my need.

It is to you my heart calls,
"Seek out my face,"
because your face, God, is what I constantly search
    for.

Don't hide your eyes from me.
Don't push away your faithful in anger.

You have always been my help.

Don't tear me out by the roots;
don't abandon me—

for you are the one I count on for help.

My father and mother may leave me,
but you have gathered me in.

Teach me, Source of Joy, your ways,
and lead me down the level plain
because of the dangers that surround me on every
      side.

Don't give me over to the breath of my fears.

For distortions have risen up in the name of truth,
they breathe out visions of destruction.

If only I could believe that I would see God's
      goodness
in the land of the living . . .

Keep up your hope in God.
Strengthen your heart and sturdy it;
keep up your hope in God.

Psalm 28

By David.

To you, God, I cry out—
don't deafen yourself to my prayer.

For if you withdraw in silence,
I will be like those who plunge into the well of
    death.

Listen to the voice of my pleading,
my cries for help when I raise up my hands
in your innermost chamber.

Don't drag me along with the wrongful,
unrepentant wreakers of harm,

those who say "peace" to their neighbors
when hatred swells in their hearts.

Repay them according to their deeds,
according to the harm they made happen.

The work of their hands,
let them feel the pain they created.

Give them what they deserve,
for they don't understand your works
or the wondrous acts of your hands.

Break them down and don't rebuild them.

I will bend my knees in praise to you
for having listened to the voice of my pleading.

You are my strength and my shield.
In you my heart trusted,
and I was helped from the dust.

My heart will exult.
I will pour out gratitude
through voice of my songs.

You give us strength;
a source of salvation
for your anointed.

Save your people; bless your possession.
Guide them like sheep,
lifting them over obstacles forever.

Psalm 29

A PSALM OF DAVID.

Praise God, all who are created in divine image.
Praise God for glory and strength.

Praise God—Wonder is the eternal name.
Bow down before the Source of Life
in witness of holy splendor.

God's voice ripples on the water.
The Source of Glory thunders,
swelling over the vastness of ocean.

Your voice is known through its power;
Your voice is heard in its splendor.

Your face splits cedars,
shattering the cedars of Lebanon.

It makes them skip like a calf,
Lebanon and Siryon,
like a wild antelope buck.

Your voice cleaves through the trees
with torch flames of fire.

It convulses the wilderness,
convulsing the wilderness of Kadesh.

Your voice pierces the terebinths,
stripping the forest bare.

And inside the holy sanctuary,
everything proclaims your glory.

You sat enthroned during the flood;
you will reign as highest forever.

You give strength to your people,
blessing them always with peace.

Psalm 30

A SONG FOR THE DEDICATION OF THE HOUSE,
BY DAVID.

I will raise you in praise, my Solace,
for you have drawn me up,
you have not let my enemies rejoice in my ruin.

God, my Physician, I cried to you for help,
and you healed me.

My Preserver, you lifted my soul from death,
kept me alive during my plunge to the pit.

Let those who love God sing out to the Source of Life,
and be thankful for memory of the holy.

For your anger lasts only a moment;
your will is in favor of life.

At night, I went to bed weeping;
in the morning—a cry of joy.

I have said in my contentment
I will never stumble.

God, only by your resolve
do I stand on mountains of strength.

When you hide your face from me,
I am confounded, confused.

To you, God, I cry out.
To my Upholder I plead for compassion.

What profit is there in my death?
In my descent to destruction?

Will the dust be thankful to you?
Will it proclaim the light of your truth?

Hear me, God, and show compassion.
My Upholder, you have always been my Source of Help.

You changed my mourning clothes to dancing,
you loosened my sackcloth and covered me with joy.

So that my depths might sing out to you and never be
    stilled,
God, my Help, I will spill out gratitude to you forever.

Psalm 31

FOR THE CONDUCTOR OF THE ETERNAL SYMPHONY,
A PSALM OF DAVID.

In you, God, I have taken refuge.
Don't let me ever fall to shame.

With your will toward goodness,
provide me means of escape.

Lean down your ear;
come to my rescue.

Be for me a Rock of strength,
a stronghold of salvation.

For you are my cliff and rest from pursuit.

In keeping with your truth,
guide me, leading me forward.

Untangle me from hidden snares.

For you are my source of sustenance.
In your hand I place my spirit for safekeeping.

Redeem me, God of truth.
I have rejected those who uphold emptiness and
    vapor.

I have put my trust in you.

I will rejoice and take pleasure in your kindness,
knowing that you have seen my affliction.

You cared for me in times of trouble,
did not surrender me to the enemy's fist.

You stood my feet on wide plains.

Treat me gently now, my Solace,
because of the narrowness of my straits.

My eye is wasted away with anger,
along with my soul and my stomach.

My life has been destroyed by grief,
my years gone down with groans.

My strength falters because of my wrongs;
my bones are eaten away.

From those who watch for my ruin, I have fallen into
    scorn,
and most of all by ones with whom I was closest.

I am a source of fear to those who know me.
Those who glimpse me in the streets flee from my face.

I have become invisible as the dead-hearted,
like a lost vessel no one bothers to look for.

For I have heard accusations of the crowd,
a whirlwind of terror all around
when they gathered together against me.

They schemed to take my life—
but I trusted in you.

I proclaimed: "You are my God.
My every instant is in your hand."

You rescued me from the grasp
of my enemies and pursuers.

Shine the light of your face upon your servant.
Save me with the strength of your kindness.

Don't let me be ashamed for calling upon you, God.
Let the wrongful fall to shame instead,
let them go to the grave in silence.

Quiet their lips of lies,
those who speak falsely against the innocent
with arrogance and scorn.

How wide is your concern!
You shelter those who revere you,
protecting all who take refuge in you from harm.

Hide them in the shelter of your presence,
away from the hard knot of people.

Conceal them in a tabernacle,
far from the contention of tongues.

Praised is God for showing me the wonder of divine
    kindness,
even in a city under siege.

I have said in my panic,
"I am cut off from before your eyes."

But you heard the voice of my plea,
the note of desperation when I cried out for help.

Love the Infinite, all who act with kindness;
the Holy One keeps watch over the faithful,
paying back in good measure those who act with pride.

Be strong and embolden your hearts,
all who long for God.

Psalm 32

By David, a psalm of understanding.

Blessed is the one who lifts up her transgressions to God;
her sins will be forgiven.

Blessed is the one for whom the Holy One
need not reckon his faults,
whose spirit is clean of deceit.

When I ploughed the fields in silence,
my bones wasted away;
they groaned all day as I worked.

For day and night your hand weighed heavy against me;
the juice of my breast went dry, like the brittle fruit of
    summer—Selah.

I made my sin known to you.
My wrongs I no longer attempted to hide.

I said, "I will confess my rebellions to God"—
and you forgave my sins and errors—Selah.

For this, let those who love you
pray at any time they can find—
do not let the flood of waters overtake them.

You are a hiding place for me,
protecting me from anguish.
You surround me with a loud cry of rescue—Selah.

I will enlighten and illumine
the path to walk.
My eyes will give witness.

Don't be like a horse,
a mule without understanding,
with a bridle and halter put on to restrain it.

In such a way God cannot approach us.

Many are the pains of those who persist in their
        wrongs,
but those who trust in their Creator are surrounded
    by love.

Take joy in God and let the righteous rejoice.
Cry out with gladness, all who are steadfast of heart.

Psalm 33

Sing out to God, all who are righteous!
To the honest, praise brings pleasure.

Thank the Holy One with the harp;
with the ten-stringed lyre make melodies.

Sing to the Source of Life a new song;
make music out of sadness
that blasts forth with joy.

For God's word is straightforward.
All divine deeds are evidence for faith.

The Holy One loves righteousness and justice;
eternal kindness flows throughout the earth.

God, with your word, the heavens were created.
With a breath of your mouth all heavenly spheres.

You gather into a heap all the seas' water,
pouring them into vaults of the deep.

Let the earth be awed by your presence
and its inhabitants be overcome by wonder.

For you spoke and it come to pass;
you commanded and your word became act.

You overturn the greed of nations,
restraining their wrongful designs.

Your counsel, Holy One, stands firm forever,
the designs of your heart from one generation to the
    next.

Happy is the nation for whom God is their Longing,
those who choose the Highest as their own.

From the heavens you gaze down
and see all who are mortal.

From the foundation where you dwell,
you take notice, Holy One,
Upholder of all who live on earth.

You are the one who shapes their hearts to unity of
    purpose,
who understands all their acts.

No king is saved by a great army.
A mighty soldier is not saved by mere strength.

A horse proves false hope when it comes to salvation.
With all its power it cannot provide means of escape.

Look! God's eye shines
upon those who revere the holy,

those who long for the divine presence—
to rescue their souls from death,
to keep them alive during famine.

Our souls wait for you,
our help and our shield.

For in you our heart rejoices.
In your holy name we have placed our trust.

May your love, God, be upon us,
whenever we long for you.

Psalm 34

>─┼─◆─○─◆┼─◄

BY DAVID, WHEN HE DISGUISED HIS PURPOSE BEFORE
    AVIMELECH,
WHO THREW HIM OUT, AND HE WALKED AWAY
    UNSCATHED.

I will bless you, God, at all times,
praise of the Highest will be constantly in my mouth.

With you, my soul shines forth glory.
When the humble hear, they will rejoice.

Come with me and praise the Creator's greatness;
let us raise the divine name together in praise.

I sought the Holy One, and I was answered.
From all my night fears, the Eternal lifted me away.

Those who look toward you stream with radiance;
their faces are never darkened by shame.

You listened when I cried out in affliction,
saving me from all that strangled tight.

Angels of God camp around those awed by wonder
to lift them from their torment away.

Taste and see—how good is our Upholder!
The one who takes refuge in you is content.

Stand in wonder, all who extol the Eternal.
There is no lack for those who hold you in awe.

Young lions crave food and are hungry,
but those who seek God never lack any good.

Come, children, listen to me.
I will teach you how to revere your Source of Joy.

Who is the one who desires life,
days of seeing only good?

Keep your tongue from speaking wrong,
your lips from duplicity.

Turn from wrong and do good.
Seek out peace and pursue it.

The eyes of the All-Knowing are upon the righteous,
the ears of the Eternal turn toward their cries.

The face of the Sustainer turns toward
    wrongdoers—
to remove their remembrance from the earth.

When the people cry out, God listens.
From all their afflictions, they are delivered safely away.

You are close to the brokenhearted;
those with crushed spirit you save.

Many are the misfortunes of the righteous,
but from all of them, you deliver them safely away.

You guard all their bones;
not one of them is broken.

Wrongdoers are killed by their own wrongs,
despisers of the righteous will eventually be brought
    to shame.

You watch tenderly, God, over your servants.
They will never be guilty,
all who take refuge in your will.

Psalm 35

By David.

Contend, God, against my contenders,
take arms against those who take arms against me.

Take hold of your shield and armor
and rise to my help.

Throw out your spear;
close yourself off to the cry of my pursuers.

Say to my soul: *I am your salvation.*

May they be ashamed and humiliated instead,
those who seek after my life.

May they be fenced off from behind;
may they dig for escape,
those who contemplate my destruction.

They will be like chaff carried on the face of the wind
with an angel of the Holy One thrusting them along
    from behind.

Their road will be dark and slippery,
with an angel of God in close pursuit.

For without cause they have hidden a trap for me.
For no reason they have dug snares for my soul.

May the dark of devastation come upon them
    suddenly.

And the trap that is hidden,
may it tangle around their legs,
bringing them down into utter dark.

My soul will exult in the Holy One,
rejoicing in divine salvation.

All my bones will declare:

God, who compares to you,
the one who lifts away the poor
from one more powerful,
the afflicted from hands of the thief?

Witnesses who crave violence rise up against me.
Those I don't know seek out my life.

They pay me back harm for good,
leaving my soul bereaved.

And I, when they were sick, wore only sackcloth.
I afflicted my soul with fasting—
may my prayer return to my breast.

As for a friend, a brother,
I paced back and forth.

As though in mourning for a mother,
I remained hunched over in darkness.

But when I limped they rejoiced and assembled;
they gathered against me to strike.

As though strangers I did not know,
they tore at me in silence.

With words of contempt,
they gnashed against me their teeth.

My Upholder, how long will you remain a bystander?
Salvage my soul from destruction.
From hungry lions keep my body intact.

I will thank you wherever people gather.
I will praise you in mighty crowds.

Don't let my enemies exult over me:
those who speak falsehood,

those who hate without cause,
whose eyes squint with cruelty.

Because they do not speak words of peace,
and for the tranquil devise words of betrayal.

They gape their mouths before me,
saying—"Ha, we have seen with our own eyes."

You have witnessed this, God—don't stay quiet.

My Upholder, don't remain distant.
Open your eyes and awaken to my cause.

My God and Sustainer, contend for me.
Judge me with fairness, One Whom I Lean On,
my Source of Help.

Don't let them rejoice over my plight.
Don't let them exclaim in their heart:
"Ha! We have triumphed."

Don't let them boast: "We have swallowed him
    whole."

Let them be ashamed and repentant,
those who delight at my downfall as one.

Let them be clothed in humiliation and
    embarrassment,
those who think themselves so high.

Then all who delight in justice
will sing out in joy.

They will proclaim at all times:
"Let us witness your infinite power,
you who take pleasure in your servant's delight."

My mouth will murmur of your righteousness,
your praises all day long.

Psalm 36

To the Conductor of the Eternal Symphony,
by a servant of God,
by David.

Transgression speaks to Restlessness in my heart.
There is no fear of God in his eyes.

Transgression speaks smoothly,
looking him straight in the eye,
saying that from his wrongs
God will hold him in eternal disdain.

The words of his mouth are heartache and lies.
He has forsaken contemplation of the good.

Even in bed, he conspires trouble.
He plants himself firmly
on a road without promise.

He refuses to refrain from wrong.

God, your kindness is in the heavens,
your faithfulness lofty as the highest clouds.

Your righteousness is tall as mighty mountains,
your justice like the great depths of sea.

Person and beast—you rescue them, God.
What a source of wealth is your kindness!

Mortals take shelter in the shadow of your wings.

They are filled to contentment with oil from your
    house.
And from the river of your delights, you give them
    drink.

Because with you is a fountain of life,
By your light we see light in the world.

Stretch out your kindness to those struggling to know
    you,
your righteousness to the straightforward of heart.

Don't let the foot of arrogance come upon me,
the hand of wrongfulness impel me forth.

There: the forces that cause sorrow have fallen.
Thrust down, they can no longer rise.

Psalm 37

BY DAVID.

Don't grow heated and angry against those who cause
    harm;
don't get jealous over those who act unjustly.

For like grass they will soon wither,
like a weed they will waste away.

Trust in God and do good;
dwell on the land,
nourishing your faith like sheep.

Delight in the Holy One,
and you will be given your heart's desire.

Reveal your path to the Eternal.
If you have trust, God will complete it,

illumining your righteousness like light,
the justice of your cause like afternoon sun.

Be silent and wait for the Creator;
don't grow heated and angry when the wrongful
succeed on their path,

those who spend their time
crafting treacherous schemes.

Calm your anger, abandon rage.
Don't grow heated; it can only bring harm.

For those who bring sorrow will be cut off;
but those who hope in God—
they will inherit the earth.

In just a little while there will be no one
who causes hurt.

You will glance at where they were,
and they will be there no longer.

But the humble will inherit the earth.
They will delight in their long contentment.

The wrongful scheme against the righteous,
gnashing against them their teeth.

My Upholder laughs,
knowing that their day will come.

Those of hatred unsheathe a sword;
pulling back the string of a bow,

aiming to bring down the afflicted and poor,
to slaughter those whose path is upright.

Their swords will pierce their own heart;
their own bow will be shattered.

What little the righteous has is good,
better than the plenty of the wrongful.

For the unjust—their arms will be broken,
but the righteous God holds upright.

The Source of Life knows the days of the innocent;
their inheritance lasts forever.

They will not be ashamed in times of trouble;
in days of famine they will always have enough.

But the wrongful will be lost,
enemies of God like smoldering meadows;
shriveled in smoke, they will vanish.

The unjust borrows but does not repay,
the righteous has compassion and gives freely.

Those God blesses will inherit the land;
and those who are cursed will be cut off.

From God our footsteps are established;
in our path, the Holy One takes delight.

Though we may fall, we are not too heavy to rise,
for the Source of Help supports our hand.

I have been a youth and I have been old,
but I have never seen those who are just forsaken

or their children seeking bread.

All day long they are generous and lend;
their offspring, for that reason, are blessed.

Turn from wrong and do good;
you will dwell in the land of promise forever.

For God loves justice,
and will not abandon the faithful,
keeping watch over them for all time.

But the seed of the wrongful will be cut off.

The righteous will inherit the land,
they will dwell upon it forever.

The one who acts rightly—her mouth
murmurs words of wisdom;
her tongue speaks softly of justice.

God's wisdom is in her heart;
her footsteps do not slide.

The seeker of harm keeps watch for her,
seeking to bring her to death.

God will not abandon the righteous
to the oppressor's hand,

will not let her come to harm
when bringing the cruel ones to judgment.

Hope for God and hold to God's path;
the Holy One will raise you up
to inherit the earth.

When the wrongful are cut off, you will witness it.

I saw a violent man who struck me with terror,
bare of branches like the fresh sapling of a tree.
Suddenly he vanished and was gone.

I sought for him but he could no longer be found.

Keep to simplicity and look straight ahead.
For the future of the righteous is contentment.

Those who rebel against God will be defeated,
all together as one.

In the end, the wrongful will be cut off.

Salvation of the righteous comes from the Creator,
their stronghold in times of fear.

God helps them and brings them to safety,
freeing them from all who cause harm—

for in the Source of Hope
they have taken shelter.

Psalm 38

A PSALM BY DAVID, A REMINDER.

God, do not rebuke me in your rage;
in the heat of your anger, do not punish me more than
    I can bear.

For your arrows have rained hard upon me;
you have brought against me heavily your hand.

There is no contentment in my flesh
because of your anger,
no peace in my bones because of my sin.

My wrongs pass over my head;
like a burden they weigh me down.

My scars are putrid and rotting,
the result of all my mistakes.

I have become twisted and distorted beyond measure.
All day long I walk in darkness—

for my loins are full of loathsome affliction.
There is no tranquility in my flesh.

I am numb, utterly crushed.
I roar from the ache in my heart.

God, all my desires are before you;
my sighing is not hidden underground.

My heart goes about like a beggar,
my strength has grown slack.

And the light of my eyes—
it is no longer with me.

My loved ones and friends
move away from my affliction,

those closest to me
stand back at a distance.

Those who seek out my life
have laid snares.

Those who hunt for my harm
speak words of destruction.
They contemplate treachery all day.

But I—like the deaf, I have not listened.
Like a mute, I did not open my mouth.

I was like one who does not hear,
in whose mouth can be found no reproof.

For you, God, I have waited.
I know you will respond, my Upholder and my God.

For I said, "Lest they rejoice,
towering above me when my leg falters."

For I am prone to stumbling;
my pain is always before my face.

I have admitted my wrongs;
I have anguished over each of my faults.

But my enemies abound with vigor and strength;
they multiply—those who hate me without cause.

Those who repay harm for good
obstruct my pursuit of contentment.

Don't forsake me, God.
My Comfort, don't grow from me distant.

Rush toward me and be my help,
my Upholder and my salvation.

Psalm 39

FOR THE CONDUCTOR OF THE ETERNAL SYMPHONY,
TO THE BELOVED, A PSALM OF DAVID.

I resolved to guard my ways;
I resolved not to blunder with my tongue.

I resolved to stifle my mouth
even when wrongdoers stood gloating before me.

I was tormented with silence.
I remained silent even in the face of good.
My pain churned turbid inside me.

Then I grew restless and irritable.
My heart grew hot within.

My mind was consumed with fire.
Finally, I let loose my tongue.

Let me know, God, my end,
and the measure of my days, what it is,
so I will know how to restrain myself.

Behold: like hairsbreadths you have parceled out my
    hours.
And my survival is accounted nothing in your sight.

Rather all is futility, all human beliefs—Selah!
Only like semblance of the living
do we walk in circles.

All our turmoil is futile.
We store up treasure,
but do not know who will harvest our reward.

And so what can I hope for, God?
I wait for you.

Since from all my rebellions you have delivered me,
with the scorn of the impious do not brand me now.

I am silent; I cannot open my mouth,
for it is you who have done this.

Take your touch from me—
by the anger of your hand, I am finished.

With rebukes of transgressions,
you chasten mortal acts.

You gnaw away like a moth
everything in which we find delight.

And so it is futile, all human beliefs—Selah.

Hear my prayer, God.
Turn your ears toward my cry for help.

Do not deafen yourself to the voice of my tears.
Because a stranger I am with you,
a sojourner like my fathers before.

Turn your gaze from me,
that I may rekindle contentment,
before I walk away and converse with you no more.

Psalm 40

For the Conductor of the Eternal Symphony,
by David, a psalm.

God, I have yearned for you,
and you leaned toward me.
You listened to my cry for help.

You lifted me up from a pit of roaring waters,
from the slippery slime of mud.

You raised my legs upon a rock,
planting my footsteps firm,

placing in my mouth a new song,
a song of praise to our Beholder.

Many see and are overcome with wonder.
They put their trust in the Source of Awe.

Happy are those who make God
their Source of Trust,

who do not turn toward self-praisers,
those seduced by lies.

Many things you have accomplished,
my God of Strength.

Your wonders and thoughts—
they are always available to us.
Nothing compares to your presence.

I will proclaim them and I will speak of them—
they are overpowering to recount.

Sacrifice and grain offerings—you do not want them.
Wanting only words, you softened toward me your ears.

A raised offering, and a mistake offering—
you never asked for them.

Then I said, "Behold, I have come,
in the scroll of the book that is written upon my
    body."

To do your will, my God, is what I have desired.
Your teaching is in my innermost parts.

I proclaimed your justice
wherever multitudes gathered.
Look! I cannot restrain my lips.

God—you—you understand.

I have not kept praise of your justice
concealed in my heart.
I have spoken of your faith and salvation.

I have not let your kindness and truth be hidden from
    the crowd.

You are the Creator—don't withhold from me your
    compassion.
Your kindness and truth—they preserve me.

The wrongs I have done surround me beyond number,
they pursue me until I can no longer see—

they are thicker than the hairs on my head—
my heart has forsaken me.

With a swift act of will, God,
lift me from harm.
My Upholder, come to my help quickly.

Let them be brought to shame,
those who seek out my life to end it.

Let them fall in embarrassment,
those who pursue my harm.

They will be desolate with loneliness,
those who gloat over others.

All who seek you will exult in joy,
They will exclaim again and again, all lovers of your
    salvation,
"May God's presence continually expand."

I am afflicted and poor—
My Upholder—consider my plight!

You are my help and means of escape.
God of Strength, do not come too late.

Psalm 41

FOR THE CONDUCTOR OF THE ETERNAL SYMPHONY,
A PSALM OF DAVID.

Blessed are those who consider the weak.
On their day of suffering,
God will give them means of escape.

The Source of Kindness will watch over them, keeping
    them alive.
They will be content on the land.

You will not relinquish their souls to obstruction
and will nourish them on the sickbed of their sadness.
The struggles of their convalescence will be made sweet.

I have said, "God, act toward me with compassion.
Heal my tormented soul, for I have wandered off
    sideways
in relation to you."

Those who despise me speak my name with scorn:
"When will he die and his name be erased?
If you go to see him, only noise does he speak.

His heart gathers sorrow like bees gather honey.
He goes outside and shouts his anguish to the clouds."

Together they whisper against me,
all who think of me little.
They conspire ways to bring harm,

saying, "Worthlessness is poured over him.
When he lies down, may he be unable to rise."

A man, a friend whom I trusted,
who ate my bread, now towers over me with his heel.

But you, God, take compassion on me; help me
    to rise—
I will make peace with those who are not peaceful.

In this I will know that you take pleasure in me:
that my enemies will be unable to cause me harm.

I—in my integrity, you have supported me.
You hold me before your presence forever.

Blessed is God, Strength of Israel,
from the beginning until the end of time.
Amen and amen.

Psalm 42

FOR THE CONDUCTOR OF THE ETERNAL SYMPHONY,
A PSALM FOR UNDERSTANDING,
BY THE OFFSPRING OF KORACH.

The way a deer longs for streams of water,
my soul has longed for you, God of Strength.

My soul has thirsted for my Upholder,
for presence of the living God.
When will I arrive and behold the light of your face?

My weeping was like bread for me—morning and
    night—
when each day they said to me, "Where is your God?"

These things I remember
and pour out my heart with my sadness—

how I passed through throngs of people,
stumbling to the holy temple,
through cries of joy and thanksgiving,
sounds of the celebrating crowd.

Why are you bent so low, my soul?
And why so in tumult over me?

Be hopeful; wait for God.

For in the future I will again thank you, my Upholder,
for turning toward me your face—
and because you are my God.

Holy One, my soul is bent low over my plight.
I will remind myself of you, then, from the land of
    Jordan,
and think of Hermon from the insignificant
mount of Mitzar.

The depths of the ocean call out to the depths
with your tunneling voice.
Your breakers and waves all crash overhead.

By day, you command kindness to accompany me,
and by night your song is at my side.

A prayer to the source of my life,
a word to the Holy One, Rock I hold on to:

Why have you forgotten me?
And why do I walk in darkness,
under threat from attack?

With words that stab through my bones,
my tormentors taunt me.
All day they say: "Where is your God?"

Why are you bent so low, my soul?
And why so in tumult?

Be hopeful; wait for God.

For in the future I will again thank you, my Upholder,
for turning toward me your face—
and because you are my God.

Psalm 43

Uphold me with justice, God;
contend my contentions
against those who are unkind.

Before one who speaks lies
and acts with injustice,
allow me means of escape.

For you, God, are my strength.
Why have you rejected me?

Why do I walk around in darkness
while my opposers press close?

Send forth your light and your truth.
They will be my guide,

bringing me to the mountain of your wonder,
place where your presence dwells.

And I will come before the holy altar,
before the Source of my Strength, rejoicing at my joy.

I will thank you with the harp,
Sustainer of the Universe, my only God.

Why are you bent so low, my soul?
And why so in tumult?

Be hopeful; wait for God.

For in the future I will again thank you, my Upholder
for turning toward me your face—
and because you are my God.

Psalm 44

FOR THE CONDUCTOR OF THE ETERNAL SYMPHONY,
BY THE OFFSPRING OF KORACH,
A PSALM OF UNDERSTANDING.

God, with our ears we have heard;
our mothers and fathers repeated the story

of deeds you performed in their days,
acts from times long ago.

You—your hand gave the people a dwelling place,
planting them in peace.

You broke nations apart
and scattered them asunder.

For not through the sword did Israel take possession
     of the land,
their arm's strength did not bring them salvation.

Rather through your right hand and muscle,
the light of your face—
for you looked on them with favor.

You are the one to whom I give all allegiance,
God of Strength—
let the remnant of Jacob be saved!

With you we can thrust down our oppressors.
With your name we can trample
wrongdoers to the ground.

For I do not trust my bow.
My sword will not bring salvation.

It is you, God, who released us from our torment.
And those who hate us, you have brought them to
     shame.

We praise you every day.
We pour out thanks to your name repeatedly—Selah.

Even so, you abandon us, leaving us disgraced;
you don't go out with our soldiers.

You made us retreat from the oppressor;
those who despise us now plunder our possessions.

You handed us over like sheep for slaughter,
scattered us among nations, seemingly without
    concern.

You sell your people, though not for wealth;
you did not even inflate their price.

You have made us a disgrace to our neighbors,
a mockery and laughingstock to those all around,

example of affliction to others,
cause for nations to shake their head.

All day long my humiliation confronts me.
My shame flushes over my face completely

from the voice of the blamer and blasphemer,
the face of the enemy and revenger.

Even though all this has happened,
we have not forgotten you.
We have not declared your covenant a lie.

Our hearts have not turned back;
our footsteps have not strayed from your path,

even though you crushed us in a land of jackals,
covered us over with shadow of death.

Have we forgotten your name, our Source of Strength?
Have we spread our hands to an unknown power?

Why don't you investigate it?
For the Holy One knows concealed things of the heart.

Out of loyalty to you, we have been killed every day.
We have been considered sheep for slaughter.

Wake up! Why do you slumber, my Upholder?
End your sleeping; don't forsake us forever.

Why do you hide your face?
You have forgotten our affliction and oppression.

Our souls are bent to the dust in prayer.
Our stomachs cling to the dirt.

Rise up! Help us!
Redeem us in keeping with your kindness.

Psalm 45

FOR THE CONDUCTOR OF THE ETERNAL SYMPHONY—
UPON THE LILY-SHAPED INSTRUMENT,
BY THE OFFSPRING OF KORACH,
A PSALM FOR UNDERSTANDING,
A SONG OF LOVE.

My heart overflows with a beautiful vision,
saying all my deeds are for sake of the king.
My tongue is the pen of a rushing scribe.

You are more lovely than any mortal.
Compassion is poured over your lips—
for that reason God will bless you forever.

Fasten a sword on your thigh, warrior.
You glow with glory and splendor.

Your spirit of majesty will triumph over harm.
Go forth and ride upon the horse of truth;
be reliant on humility and justice,

let your right hand,
guide you toward justice.

Your muscle's strength inspires awe.

Your arrows are sharp; nations fall beneath you,
along with the hearts of all who oppose your will.

Your throne, established by God, is eternal.

Your staff is straightforward,
the staff of your guidance.

You have loved what is right,
despised what is wrong.

For this the Holy One, your God, has anointed you,
chosen you with oil of rejoicing from among all your
      friends.

Myrrh, aloes, and cassia—your clothing smells of
      them.
From ivory palaces, the melody of lutes gives you
      pleasure.

The daughters of kings visit you.
Ravishing queens stand at your right
clothed in the gold of Ophir.

Listen, daughter, and look;
strain to hear.

Forget your people and your father's house.
The king is wild in desire over your beauty.

Because he is God's messenger,
bow down before his love.

Daughter of Tyre,
the wealthy have been sick with longing
upon beholding the gift of your face.

All the glory of the king's chosen one
is revealed within the palace gates;
Her clothing is woven with gold.

Covered in embroidery, she will be carried to the king.
Virgins will be brought afterward, her friends.

They are brought with joy and exultation;
they enter the palace of the king.

Your children will be like their father.
You will make them royalty throughout the land.

Your name I will make a remembrance in every
    generation.
The people will thank you forever and beyond.

Psalm 46

FOR THE CONDUCTOR OF THE ETERNAL SYMPHONY,
BY THE OFFSPRING OF KORACH,
BY THE YOUNG WOMEN, A SONG.

God, you are for us a strength and a shelter—
in times of affliction,
you are found everywhere we look.

And so we won't be afraid
at changes of the earth,

when mountains tumble into the heart of the sea
or waters rage with tumultuous froth;

the peaks quake in awe of your presence—Selah.

A river—its streams will bring rejoicing to your city.
Holy are the dwelling places of the Most High.

With you in its midst, it will not totter;
you change its darkness to dawn.

Nations rage tumultuous; governments totter.
When you give forth voice, the earth melts.

The Creator of the Heavenly Array is with us,
the Upholder of Jacob will keep us from harm—
    Selah.

Come and gaze at God's works,
the one who has astounded the world with wonders,
who has brought all the earth's wars to a halt.

The bow will be shattered and the arrow split in half,
the chariot burnt in fire.

Be calm and know that I am your Sustainer.

I will be lifted in praise among nations,
I will be lifted in praise throughout the earth.

The Creator of the Heavenly Array is with us,
The Upholder of Jacob will keep us from harm—
    Selah.

Psalm 47

FOR THE CONDUCTOR OF THE ETERNAL SYMPHONY,
BY THE OFFSPRING OF KORACH, A PSALM.

Clap your hands, all nations!
Trumpet a cry of exultation to God!

For the Exalted One fills us with wonder
from the highest heavens
throughout the earth.

You speak to nations on our behalf,
countries where we place our feet.

You have chosen us for your own,
the beauty of Jacob, whom you love—Selah.

You rise with a blast of the trumpet!
You are heard in the voice of the shofar!

Sing out to the Holy One, sing out!
Sing out to the one who gives us direction, sing out!
For God is sovereign over all the earth.

Make a melody of your understanding.

God reigns over nations;
God sits on a holy throne.

Those who give freely
gather together in praise,
people of the God of Abraham.

For to you belong all who protect the earth;
your Holy Presence is lifted high beyond measure.

Psalm 48

A SONG, A PSALM BY THE OFFSPRING OF KORACH.

God is vast and deeply praised—
in the city of our Upholder,
upon the holy mountain.

The view from there is beautiful,
bringing joy to all the earth.

The mountain of Zion,
northern flank of Jerusalem,
city of the Incomparable Power, God—

its palaces are known as a refuge.

For look! The leaders joined forces.
They marched toward its walls together as one.

When they saw it, they were struck into silence.
They were paralyzed by fright,

seized with trembling,
writhing like a woman giving birth.

In the eastern wind,
God shattered the ships of Tarshish.

What they heard of, they witnessed firsthand—
in the city of the one who orders the heavens,

city of our Deepest Hope,
God of Strength, may you sustain it forever—Selah.

We are awed speechless, Source of Life,
by your kindness, as we stand in your temple.

The praise of you, God, is like your name.
It reaches the ends of earth.

Righteousness fills your right hand.
Let the mountain of Zion rejoice.
Let the daughters of Judah exult at your justice.

Walk around Zion, trace its circumference.
Count its towers,
Set your heart to comprehending its strength.

Walk between its citadels,
so you can tell of it to the next generation.

Because of this, the Holy One, our God,
will continue forever, into the World to Come.

You will lead us even beyond death.

Psalm 49

For the Conductor of the Eternal Symphony,
by the offspring of Korach, a psalm.

Listen to this, all nations.
Bend down your ears, all who live under sharp knife
    of time—

tillers of soil as well as offspring of the wealthy,
those of elevated station along with those who barely
    survive.

My mouth speaks words of wisdom;
my heart murmurs insights acquired firsthand.

I lean out my ear for parables;
I search out my puzzlement with a lyre.

Why should I fear days of calamity,
when the injustice of my pursuers engulfs me—

those who trust in their riches
and for their great abundance praise only themselves?

People who will not redeem their own brothers,
who will not come to God with atonement,

the ransom of their soul is too high.
They die, then, for all eternity.

Can a person live as though immortal
and not see muscles weaken and flesh decay?

No, we see that the wise ones perish,
along with the foolish and brutish, who are lost to an
    abyss.

Their wealth is relinquished to others,
their grave is their eternal home,

their dwelling place from one generation to the next.
You can read their names upon the earth.

Nobody lies down to sleep with their riches.
Before God, we are all like silent beasts of the field.

Such is the path of the foolish,
they rush after their own pleasure—Selah.

Like flocks of sheep, their end is the underworld.
Death will graze on the flesh of their bones.

Those who follow the straight and humble path
will descend to them in the morning.

They will see shapes of bodies withered from dwelling
   in the grave,
fallen from their lofty abode.

But God will redeem my life from the underworld,
taking me into the holy presence—Selah.

Do not be struck with fear when others grow rich,
when their houses grow heavy from the weight of
   their wealth.

For they cannot take all their possessions to the grave;
the weight of their wealth will not follow them down.

Though their spirit while alive may be blessed,
they should be grateful to you, God, for giving them
   such good.

They will come the way of all before them,
those who will never open their eyes to light again.

All mortals are visitors and do not understand;
we are all like silent animals before the will of God.

Psalm 50

A SONG, BY ASAF.

The Holy Creator, Source of Strength and Eternal
    Life, spoke,
calling out to all the earth—
from the eastern sunrise to the place of its setting.

From Zion, the fulfillment of beauty,
God shone forth.

When our Upholder comes, it will not be quiet.
A consuming fire will ravage in front.
The air all around will shudder with storm.

God will call to the sky above
and to the earth to hold the people on trial.

Gather to me all the devoted ones,
those who uphold my covenant through offerings.

Let the heavens speak of God's righteousness,
justice of the eternal judge—Selah.

Hear, my people, and I will speak,
Listen, Israel, and I will bear witness to your strife.

I am the Holy One, your God.
It is not for lack of sacrifices that I rebuke you,

Your offerings are constantly before my eyes.

I do not need bulls from your house,
rams from your flocks of sheep.

For mine is every beast in the forest,
cattle of a thousand mountains.

I know the name of every bird on the hillsides;
the creatures of the field I hold constantly before
   my eyes.

Even if I were hungry, I would not ask for food,
for every continent is mine and all that fills it.

Do I need flesh of bulls to quiet my hunger?
Does blood of rams quench my thirst?

The only sacrifice I need is your gratitude;
fulfillment of your oaths to the Most High.

When you call upon me during days of difficulty
I will draw you out from pits of despair;
then you will behold my glory.

And to the unjust, God said:
What right do you have to speak of my laws?

To repeat my statutes?
To mouth my covenant with your lips?

You who despise rebuke,
throwing my words behind you like trash?

If you see a thief, you want to be like him;
when you see adulterers you think it not such a bad
      idea.

You have sent forth your mouth to spread hatred,
your tongue is a necklace of lies.

You sit with your brothers and speak against me,
with your mother's children and point out my flaws,

These things you have done, and I remained silent.
You imagined I didn't care.

Now I will straighten you out, arranging the details
      before your eyes.

I ask you to understand, you who have forgotten how
      to be holy,
lest it is all destroyed and there is none to bring
      respite.

The one who sacrifices gratitude pays me the only true
      tribute,
Pay attention to the road:
I will illumine to you the visible salvation of God.

Psalm 51

FOR THE CONDUCTOR OF THE ETERNAL SYMPHONY,
A PSALM OF DAVID,
WHEN NATHAN THE PROPHET CAME TO HIM
UPON HIS RETURN FROM BATSHEVA.

Give to me, God,
in accordance with your kindness.

In keeping with your compassion,
erase my acts of revolt.

Wash from me my wrongfulness.
From my imperfect acts, make me again pure.

For I know my transgressions;
my mistakes are always before my eyes.

Against you alone have I failed.
What is wrong in your sight,
I have done it.

So you are right with your words;
your lips speak the truth.

With instinct for wrongfulness, I was born.
With inclination toward error,
I burst forth from the womb.

Is it true that you desire trust?
Then teach me the secret of wisdom.

Scrub my straying with hyssop and I will again be
  pure.
Cleanse me and I will be whiter than snow.

Let me once more hear joy and gladness,
let the bones you have crushed know delight.

Hide your eyes from my mistakes;
erase all my wrongs.

Create for me a pure heart, Holy One;
renew in me a spirit of purposeful direction.

Don't cast me away from you.
And the spirit of your holiness,
don't take it from me away.

Return to me joy at your salvation;
let a generous spirit sustain my life.

I will teach transgressors your path;
the mistaken will turn back toward your service.

Lift me away from bloodstain,
Eternal One, God of my salvation.
My tongue will cry out in praise of your justice.

My Upholder, open my lips,
and my mouth will proclaim your praise.

For you do not desire sacrifice, or I would give it.
You do not crave a burnt offering.

The only true sacrifice to God is a broken spirit,
a crushed and shattered heart—
that you will not despise.

Bring goodness to Zion in keeping with your will;
build up Jerusalem's walls.

Then you will again desire sacrifices of the righteous,
burnt offerings and contributions wholly consumed.

Only then can they offer bulls on your altar.

Psalm 52

FOR THE CONDUCTOR OF THE ETERNAL SYMPHONY,
A SONG OF UNDERSTANDING, BY DAVID,
WHEN DOEG THE EDOMITE CAME BEFORE SAUL
AND SAID TO HIM, "DAVID HAS ARRIVED AT THE HOUSE
   OF ACHIMELECH."

Why do you congratulate yourselves
over the wrong committed by might?
God's kindness exists all day long.

Your tongue devises chasms of destruction,
like a blade sharpened to work its betrayal.

You love wrong more than good,
lies more than justice—Selah.

You have loved adorning all your words with deceit,
sworn allegiance to a tongue of deception.

For this, the Eternal will pull you down,
breaking your strength completely,

tearing you from your tent,
loosening your roots from land of the living—Selah.

The righteous will see and be filled with wonder,
overflowing with joy at divine justice.

"Look at the warrior who didn't make
God his source of strength!

He trusted in his abundance of riches,
grew strong through destruction."

But I am like a fresh olive in the house of the Creator.
I have trusted the Holy One's love to accompany me
in this world and the next.

I will thank God for the world, the one who made it;
I will put hope in the holy name—

emblem of goodness
to all who are faithful.

Psalm 53

FOR THE CONDUCTOR OF THE ETERNAL SYMPHONY,
UPON FALLING SICK,
A PSALM OF UNDERSTANDING,
BY DAVID.

The walking corpse says in his heart:
"There is no God."

They ravage and abominate themselves,
bringing about sorrow.
There is no one who labors for good.

The Holy One looks down upon humanity
to see if there exists a person of understanding,
one who seeks out divine truth.

All of them have turned away;
together, like one, they have grown rancid.

There is no one who labors for good,
not even one.

Do you not know, all workers of harm,
you who devour my people
as though devouring bread,
you who don't call out to your Upholder—

wherever you are, you will be gripped with great fear,
even when source of terror does not exist.

For God has scattered the bones
of those who camp against the faithful.

The Holy One will fill them with shame,
for they are turned away from the Source of Life.

Who will bring salvation to Israel from Zion?
When God returns his people from captivity,
Jacob will exult; Israel will cry out with joy.

Psalm 54

FOR THE CONDUCTOR OF THE ETERNAL SYMPHONY,
UPON MUSICAL INSTRUMENTS,
A PSALM OF UNDERSTANDING, BY DAVID,
WHEN THE ZIPPHINITES CAME AND SAID TO SAUL,
"IS NOT DAVID HIDING AMONG US?"

God, with your name, save me;
with your muscle come to my defense.

Holy One, hear my prayer,
give ear to the utterance of my mouth.

For strangers have risen against me,
those who cause trembling seek out my life.

They have not placed you before their face—Selah.

Behold—God helps me!
My Strength is with those who uphold my life.

The Eternal will return wrong to those who watch
    for my weakness.

With your truth, annihilate them into silence—

I will sacrifice to you freewill offerings,
I will pour out thanks to your name—for it is good.

You have lifted me away from all trouble.

In the midst of enemies,
I can look them straight in the eye.

Psalm 55

For the Conductor of the Eternal Symphony,
upon musical instruments, a song of
    understanding, by David.

Open your ears to my prayer, O God.
Don't hide yourself from my pleading.

Listen with compassion and respond to my cry.
My words leave me restless, unsettled—

because of the enemy's voice,
because of the wrongful compressing against me,

for they thrust me into anguish,
and with their anger, persist in their grudge.

My heart convulses inside;
fear of death has fallen on my soul.

Terror and trembling flood through me;
I am overtaken with shudders.

I say:

Who will give me wings like the dove?
I would fly off and dwell someplace else.

Know that I would go far in my wandering.
I would sleep in the desert—Selah.

I would rush toward escape
from raging wind, from insanity's storm.

Swallow them, God, confuse their tongues.
For I have witnessed violence and strife in the city.

Day and night, they surround its walls,
stirring up trouble, causing torment within,
leaving a swath of destruction in their wake.

Harm and hypocrisy never leave its streets.

For it is not an enemy who reviles me;
I could bear that.

It is not one I hate who has magnified himself above
    me—
I could hide from such a one.

But it is my soul's companion, one of my measure,
one I looked up to, my intimate friend—

with whom I conversed about the sweetness of the
    mystery.
We used to walk together to the house of God to
    pray.

May you place the shroud of death upon such
    people.
May they be hurled to the underworld alive.

For evils multiply inside them,
accompanying them wherever they dwell.

I cry out to God and am answered—
evening, morning, and afternoon.

I weep and I moan,
but the Holy One listens to my voice,

redeeming my soul with tranquility
from the battle that rages within—
for those same people were once on my side.

God, hear me and humble them;
you are the Creator who has ruled from the
 beginning—Selah.
You will never vanish—and still, they do not hold you
 in awe.

My friend lifted his hand
against one who brought only well wishes;
he profaned our unspoken accord.

His mouth was smooth as butter,
but inside his heart was all war.

His words were softer than oil,
but they were doorways to what lay underneath.

Those who cast their cares upon the Creator will be
 sustained.
The Holy One will not let the righteous stumble forever.

And you, God, hurl them into a pit of destruction.

People of blood and lies, they worry
over the portion of their days.

But as for me, I put all my trust in you.

Psalm 56

For the Conductor of the Eternal Symphony,
upon seeing the silent dove who flies into the
    distance,
by David, a song like gold,
when the Philistines captured him in Gath.

Turn toward me with compassion, God of Justice,
for a mortal pants in pursuit of me all day—
battling against me, pressing down hard.

Those who watch for my downfall
are vigilant, waiting for their chance to crush.

For many are my contenders; they raise themselves
    up high.

When I grow afraid, I turn my trust toward you.
In the Source of Justice—I praise your word.

In my Protector I have trusted; I will not fear.
What can a mere mortal do to me?

All day my words are saturated with sadness.
Upon me my contenders
heap only thoughts of harm.

They have stirred up against me,
crouching, waiting to pounce.

They are like my heels—following me wherever I walk,
seeking to end my life.

Take them away from their tormenting.
In your anger, whole nations are brought to the
    ground.

You have counted my fugitive wanderings.
You emptied my tears into your flask—
have you not recorded their measure?

Then let my pursuers turn from me
on the day I cry out for compassion.

This I know: that you are on my side.

The Source of Justice—I praise your word.
The God of Transcendence—I praise your speech.

In my Protector I have trusted; I will not fear.
What can a mere mortal do to me?

Upon myself, God, I place vows of allegiance.
I will repay you with a grateful heart.

For you have saved my soul from death,
have not let my legs stumble to destruction—

so that I might walk before God in the salvaged light
    of the living.

Psalm 57

FOR THE CONDUCTOR OF THE ETERNAL SYMPHONY,
A PLEA TO BE SPARED DESTRUCTION,
BY DAVID, A SONG LIKE GOLD,
WHEN HE FLED BEFORE SAUL INTO A CAVE.

Be kind to me, God, be soft.
Because with you my soul's blood finds
    protection;

in the shadow of your wings, I will wrap
    myself
until the storm of devastation has passed.

I will call out to you, the Highest,
the one who makes my journey's road complete.

You send down help from the heavens and save me
from the autumn chill that breathes down my back—
    Selah.

You send forth kindness and truth.

Oh, but my soul is surrounded by lions,
I lie down with those who burn and flame.

Their teeth are spears and arrows,
their tongue a sharpened sword.

Raise yourself above the heavens, God;
spread over all the earth is your glory.

They prepared a trap for my footsteps;
my life was bent and broken.

They dug a pit before me
and fell into it themselves—Selah.

My heart is turned toward you, God,
my heart is steady in direction.

I will sing to you and make melodies to your name.
Awake, my innermost glory!
Awake, O lyre and harp!

With you I will awaken the dawn.

I will cry out thanks to you, my Upholder,
before all people,
sing your praises to all nations.

For expansive as the heavens is your kindness,
transcendent as the clouds is your truth.

Raise yourself above the heavens, God.
Spread over all the earth is your glory.

Psalm 58

FOR THE CONDUCTOR OF THE ETERNAL SYMPHONY,
A PLEA TO BE SPARED DESTRUCTION,
BY DAVID, A PSALM LIKE GOLD.

Is it true, silent One, that you speak of righteousness?
Do you really judge with fairness humankind?

Even while their hearts offer sacrifice,
their hands weigh out violence in the land.

The wrongful are estranged from you from the womb.
Those who speak falsely stumble since birth.

Their heat is like a feverish snake;
like a deaf cobra, they plug their ears.

They don't hear the voice of those whispering wisdom,
friends who try to help.

God of Justice, smash their teeth in their mouths.
Pull out the fangs of the lions.

They will melt like water, trickling themselves away.
The wrongful aim the arrows of their speech
to plunge beneath the skin.

Like a snail that oozes as it moves,
like a woman's stillbirth that never glimpses the sun.

Until they understand, they will be tangled in thorns.
Upon my life, God's fury will rage like a storm.

The righteous will rejoice when they see recompense
    of the wrongful.
They will wade through their blood.

People will say:

So there is indeed fruit for the righteous.
So there *is* a God who judges all the earth.

Psalm 59

FOR THE CONDUCTOR OF THE ETERNAL SYMPHONY,
A PLEA TO BE SPARED DESTRUCTION,
BY DAVID, A SONG LIKE GOLD,
WHEN SAUL SENT MEN
TO KEEP WATCH AT HIS HOUSE AND KILL HIM.

Lift me from my enemies, God.
From those who rise up against me,
raise me beyond reach.

Pull me away from those who work for destruction,
from those thirsting for blood, be my rescue.
For—look!—they lie in ambush for my soul.

The unflinching gather against me—
not for my transgression, God of Forgiveness;
I have not sinned.

Though I am not guilty, they rush toward me,
hungry to kill.

Wake up and stand witness!
You are the Holy One, Creator of the Heavenly Array,
     God of Israel.

Raise yourself from sleep; keep watch over all the
     people.
Do not relent against traitors who cause harm—Selah.

They return each evening, growling like dogs;
they surround the city.

Look! Their mouths foam.
Their lips are swords.

They say, "Who is listening?"

But you, God, you laugh,
making light of them before the nations.

Their power is so strong! But I keep watch for you,
for you are my place of refuge.

Source of Kindness, come closer;
show me my hidden foes.

Don't kill them lest my people forget.

Make them stagger with your might, bringing them
    down.
Be for us a shield, my Upholder.

The wrongs of their mouths,
the words on their lips—

they will be taken captive by their own pride,
by the curse and deception they speak.

Extinguish them in your fury.
Extinguish them so they exist no more.

And it will known that the God of Justice guides
    Jacob
until the ends of the earth—Selah.

They return each evening, growling like dogs.
They surround the city.

They wander in search of food;
still hungry, they lie down to sleep.

But I will sing of your strength;
I will cry out your kindness each morning.

For you have been a place of comfort for me,
a refuge to flee toward when troubles approach.

My Solace, it is to you I make melodies—
for you are my tower of strength,
my Healer, a source of eternal kindness.

Psalm 60

⊱┈╌∘╌┈⊰

FOR THE CONDUCTOR OF THE ETERNAL SYMPHONY,
UPON THE LILY-SHAPED INSTRUMENT,
A TESTIMONY,
A SONG LIKE GOLD, BY DAVID,
A WELLSPRING OF TEACHING,
WHEN HE STRUGGLED WITH
ARAM OF THE TWO RIVERS AND ARAM OF THE SWOLLEN
   PLAINS,
AND YOAV RETURNED AND STRUCK EDOM
IN THE VALLEY OF SALT
ALONG WITH AN ARMY OF TWELVE THOUSAND.

God, you have spurned us.
You have broken against us in anger.
Now, help us return to your arms.

You have caused the land to quake,
splitting it open.
Heal its cracks, for it has grown unsturdy.

You made your people suffer hardship.
The wine you gave us makes us reel.

But you have given those who hold you in wonder
a sign to hold on to: your truth—Selah.

Release your loved ones from suffering;
stretch out your right arm in response!

God spoke with holiness:
I will exult as I divide Shechem;
I will measure out the Valley of Booths.

Gilead is mine, and mine is Menashe.
Ephraim is the strength of my head.
Judah is my eternal portion.

Moav is the pot I wash in.
Upon Edom, I throw my shoe.
Upon Philistine, I break myself.

Who will lead me to the city under siege?
Who will lead me to Edom?

Why have you spurned us, God?
Why don't you go out with our troops?

Give us help from all that troubles us.
Useless is salvation from humankind.

With God we become strong.
It is the Holy One who will trample our oppressors to
    the ground.

Psalm 61

><+>-0-<+><

FOR THE CONDUCTOR OF THE ETERNAL SYMPHONY,
WITH MUSICAL INSTRUMENTS, BY DAVID.

Listen, God, to my weeping.
Be attentive to the words of my prayer.

From the end of the earth, I call to you
when my heart grows faint within.

When a rock is lifted high above, you guide me,
for you have been my shelter,
a tower of strength amidst all that confronts me.

I would dwell in your tent forever,
taking shelter in the protection of your wings—Selah.

For you, God, listen to my vows.
You give testimony to those who revere your name.

You have added days to the life of the king,
increased his years from generation to generation.

May he dwell before God's face forever
with love and kindness as the manna that preserves
    him.

For that, I will always make melodies to your name,
fulfilling my vows from day to day.

Psalm 62

><+<>+○+<>+<

FOR THE CONDUCTOR OF THE ETERNAL SYMPHONY,
TO THE BELOVED, A PSALM OF DAVID.

In the face of the Creator alone, my soul is silenced;
my salvation comes from the Source of Life.

Only God is my Rock and salvation,
my high place of refuge;
with my Upholder I will not stumble much.

How long will you fall upon a man?
You will slay yourselves, all of you.

You are like a leaning wall,
a fence crumbling under its own weight.

For loftiness alone
they conspired to bring me down.

They delight in deception;
with their mouths they bless
but inwardly they curse—Selah!

Only God is my Rock and salvation—
my high place of refuge;
with the Holy One I will not stumble.

God is my salvation and my glory,
Rock of my strength, one I turn to for help.

Trust the Source of Life at all times, O people,
pour out the contents of your heart.

God is our shelter—Selah.

In truth, humanity is nothing but vapor;
an illusion they are, all the children of women and
    men.

Weighed on the scales, all of them together,
they are lighter than breath.

Do not trust those who wield emblems of power;
do not empty yourselves in plunder.

Though wealth bears fruit,
don't give to it the entirety of your heart.

One thing God has spoken;
these two I have heard:

true strength comes from the Creator,
and you, my Upholder, provide kindness.

For you bring all people contentment
according to the wealth of their deeds.

Psalm 63

A PSALM BY DAVID, WHEN HE WAS IN THE WILDERNESS
OF JUDAH.

Holy One, you are my Source of Strength.
I search for you at dawn.

My throat thirsts for you.
My flesh faints for your presence
in a land parched and empty,
utterly without water.

In holy places, I have gazed for you,
hoping to witness your power and glory,
for your kindness is better than life.

My lips will praise you;
I will bless you with my entire life.

When I speak your name, I will lift up my hands.
As with richness and oil, my soul will be sated,
my lips will sing out with love—

when I think of you while lying in bed,
when I contemplate you during the night watches
and realize it is you who have been my help—
from the shadow of your wings I cry out with joy.

My soul cleaves to your presence,
for your right hand holds me up.

Those who seek to end my life in violence,
they will fall into the deepest recesses of the earth.

Their blood will be poured out by the sword.
They will be food for the jackals.

The king will rejoice in the Eternal.
All those who have sworn allegiance to the Holy One
will shine forth with praise

until the mouths of your detractors
stop speaking lies.

Psalm 64

FOR THE CONDUCTOR OF THE ETERNAL SYMPHONY,
A PSALM OF DAVID.

Listen to my voice, God, when I speak;
from fear of the enemy, preserve my life.

From the plot of the wrongful, keep me well hidden,
from tumult of those who bring sorrow,

those who sharpen their tongues like a sword,
who pull back their arrow with a bitter word—

to shoot from concealment the innocent.
They aim suddenly, having no fear;

they grab hold with a hurtful phrase;
they speak a language hidden with traps.

They think, who will see?
They search for everyone's faults.

They search everything that can be searched,
each innermost soul, each heart's deepest valley.

God will shoot them suddenly with an arrow;
its point will strike flesh.

Their tongues will make them stumble.
All who see them will take to flight.

They will fear everyone
until they speak of God's work
and become enlightened about creation.

The one who acts rightly will rejoice in the Holy
    One,
taking refuge in the divine source of comfort.

All who are straightforward of heart
will shine forth with praise.

Psalm 65

FOR THE CONDUCTOR OF THE ETERNAL SYMPHONY,
A PSALM BY DAVID, A SONG.

To you silence is praise, O God in Zion,
and to you all vows are fulfilled.

One Who Listens to Prayer,
to you all flesh comes.

My wrongs overwhelm me,
but our rebellions—you always forgive them.

Blessed are those whom you choose to draw near to;
they dwell in your courtyards.

We will be fed to contentment with the abundance of
    your house,
the holiness of your innermost sanctuary.

Your wonders give us insight to justice,
God of our salvation,

the One who can be trusted
from the ends of the earth
to the far distant seas,

who establishes mountains in place with power,
who is shielded with strength.

The one who soothes the roaring of the seas,
the rage of their waves,
the tumult of nations.

Those who live at the ends of the earth
are awed by your presence.

You bring forth daylight and make the dusk cry out
    with joy.
You keep watch over the earth, giving it drink;
you beautify it all beyond measure.

Your streambed is full of water.
You provide the people with grain,
for that is your resolve.

You water the jagged mountains,
quenching their thirst.

They soften with spring rain;
you bless its new growth.

You crown the year with abundance.
Your pastures drip with oil;
meadows flow with springs.

The hills exult, surrounded by water.
They clothe themselves with flocks of sheep;
the valleys are blanketed with grain.

Nature cries out in delight; it sings.

Psalm 66

For the Conductor of the Eternal Symphony,
  a song, a psalm.

Burst forth with joy, all the earth!
Sing to the glory of God's name,
make glory the form of your praise.

Say to the Holy One: How wondrous are your deeds!
When they see the vastness of your power,
even your enemies pretend to obey.

All earth bows down, singing your name.
They make melodies in praise of your nature—Selah.

Go and look at the works of the Creator.

Your acts provoke awe beyond anything humans
    attain.
You turned the sea into dry land;
they crossed through the river on foot.

Once free, we rejoiced in your presence.

Your steadfast power is always apparant;
your eyes stare into the nations' depths.

The rebellious will not rise up against you—Selah.

Bless the wonder and grandeur of God, O nations.
With full voice, let the Creator's praise be heard—

the one who sparked our soul to life,
who did not allow our feet to stumble.

For you tested us, God.
You smelted us as through silver.

You brought us like prisoners to a stronghold,
binding our loins tightly.

You let a mortal ride a chariot over our heads.
We survived through fire and water—
in the end, you led us out to drink our fill.

I will come to your house with offerings of ascent,
I will fulfill to you all my vows—

even ones that burst through my lips,
that my mouth spoke in times of constriction.

I will offer you fattened calves,
sweet-smelling smoke of rams,
oxen along with goats—Selah.

Come, listen, all those awed by God,
and I will tell you
what the Holy One did for my soul.

To my Protector my mouth cried out,
but praise remained under my tongue.

Wrongfulness—if I had seen it in my heart,
my Upholder would not have listened to me.

And yet, God, you have listened.
In times past, you paid attention to my pleas.

Praised are you who have not turned from my prayer,
nor turned your kindness from me.

Psalm 67

For the Conductor of the Eternal Symphony,
on the stringed instrument, a melody, a song.

God, treat us gently,
and we will kneel before you in praise.

Light up your face so we can see it—Selah—

to make your path known to the earth;
your saving power to all the nations.

People will pour out gratitude to you;
people will pour out gratitude, all of them.

Countries will rejoice, crying out with praise.

For you judge all people with clarity;
you guide all countries of the earth—Selah.

People will pour out gratitude to you.
People will pour out gratitude, all of them.

The land offers forth its crop—

the Creator, our God, has blessed us,
and will continue to bless
until the ends of the earth hold you in awe.

Psalm 68

FOR THE CONDUCTOR OF THE ETERNAL SYMPHONY,
BY DAVID, A PSALM, A SONG.

Rise up, God, scatter all who obstruct you,
let those who reject your truth flee before your face.

As smoke is swallowed into air, diffuse them.

The way wax melts before fire,
so are the wrongful lost from beholding your gaze.

The righteous celebrate,
exulting before your presence.

They erupt with joy.

Sing out to our Source of Hope; make melodies to the
    Holy Name;
Lift up a song for the great chariot driver in the desert—
to the Infinite One, exulting before our Upholder.

Parent to orphans and defender of widows,
God dwells in a holy chamber.

The Source of Justice settles the lonely into houses,
leading prisoners toward lives that are fruitful.

Only those who turn from your presence
dwell in sweltering sun—

God, you go out before your people,
you march beside them in wasteland—Selah.

The earth started to quake, even the sky wept
before your presence at Sinai;
from gaze of the Holy One, God of Israel.

Our Provider gives forth a generous drizzle of rain.
The river and weary soil, the Creator renews them.

Our livestock dwell on it.
God, with your goodness you help the afflicted endure.

My Upholder, you give your word.

The women who bring forth blessing will be a great
    multitude,
but oppressive rulers of legions will flee, they will flee.

The woman of the house will divide her wealth
with maidservants who sleep near the fire.

If you have dwelt on ground of darkness, you will rise—
like wings of the dove gilded with silver,
pinions brilliant with emerald gold.

When God's presence spreads over kings,
snow will come to realms of shadow.

The mountain of the Holy One is the Mount of Bashan;
its pastures make for good grazing.

The mountain of summits is the Mount of Bashan;
its ridges make it stretch high.

Why do you tremble, ridges of high summit,
mountain chosen for God's abode,
ground where the Holy One will settle forever?

Chariot riders who accompany the Creator are tens
    of thousands,
a myriad of angels on high, and my Upholder is with
    them,
with them upon Sinai in holiness.

You have risen to the heights;
you have returned us from captivity,
accepting gifts from humankind.

Even the rebellious can dwell
with the Holy One, God of Justice.

Praised is the Eternal from day to day,
the One who carries our burden, God of our
    salvation—Selah.

The Creator, for us, is the Strength of salvation.
God, my Upholder, leading us out from even death.

Our Protector will smash down the enemy,
the forehead of those who walk unconcerned in their
    guilt.

My Upholder said: *From Bashan I will return.*
I will return from the depths of the sea.

to redden your enemies' feet with blood;
your dogs' tongues will lick up its puddle.

Look at God's pathways.
The roads of the Creator, my Strength, are all holy.

Singers approach in the wake of musicians,
in the midst of young women playing their drums.

Praise God in holy congregations,
celebrate My Upholder from the wellspring of Israel.

There Benjamin, the youngest, took power,
but chiefs of Judah stoned them,
followed by leaders of Zevulun and Naftali.

You tell us to keep strength,
strength of the God of Justice.

This you have done for us, our Protector,
from your palace in Jerusalem.
To you the kings offer gifts.

Rebuke the creatures that swarm in the swamp reed,
bulls that trample the weak calves of nations,
those who stampede with lust for silver.

Scatter the nations, the ones who work only toward
    wars.

The well-fed will come from Egypt.
Cush will hasten its hand
to serve the Source of Eternal Life.

Kingdoms of the earth, sing out to God,
make melodies to my Upholder—Selah.

The one who rides on the highest eastern heaven.
The one whose strength speaks in a clear voice.

Proclaim the power of the Almighty.

Upon Israel is God's majesty;
divine strength floats through fine particles of cloud.

Awesome is the Creator from the place of holiness,
the Eternal Strength of Israel,
one who gives power and strength to the people.

Praise God.

Psalm 69

For the Conductor of the Eternal Symphony,
a song on the lily-shaped instrument, by David.

Save me, God of Creation,
because the waters are up to my throat,

I am sunk in swamps of sun-flickered depths
and can find for my legs no foothold.

I have been swallowed by valleys of water,
and the streams have washed me away.

By my own pleading I have grown weary.
My throat is dry with terror, my eyes grown weak
from waiting for my Heavenly Protector.

More abundant than the hairs on my head
are those who seek without reason my harm.

Like bones without flesh are those who wish me
    extinction,
forces of wrong that speak of me falsely.

Even though I have not stolen, I repay them what they
    demand.

God, you know my foolhardy ways,
and my guilty acts are not concealed from your face.

Don't let those who hope for you become
    disheartened
when they see my plight.

My Upholder, you are God of those who serve you.
Let those who seek you not be made
through my example ashamed.

O God of the people Israel!
For your sake I have carried scorn.
Loss of dignity covers my face.

I have become loathsome to my brothers,
a stranger to my mother's sons.

Through zeal for your house I have been devoured;
scorn of those who scorn you has fallen on my head.

I wept while my soul grew weak with fasting.
Your refusal to answer was a constant taunt.

And so I dressed only in sackcloth;
I became for others the subject of cruel jokes.

They gossiped about me, those who sit at the gate—
a song of derision, by those who drink to delirium.

I am my prayer to you, God—
may it always be a time of favor.

Eternal One, answer me with your kindness,
with the truth of your salvation.

Save me from the mire; don't let me sink.
Deliver me from those who seek out my harm;
lift me up from deep valleys of water.

Don't let floodstreams of water rise over my head.
Don't let the deepest ocean rise up to my throat.
Don't let the well close over my eyes.

Answer me, God, for your kindness is good.
Because your compassion is infinite,
turn toward me the light of your face.

Don't hide your countenance
from one trying to serve your will.
Because I am tormented, answer me quickly.

Draw close to me; deliver me.
Because my enemies surround me,
lift me from harm.

You know of my humiliation, embarrassment, disgrace.
Before you stands all that I fear.

Humiliation has broken my heart; I am sickened to
    death.
I longed for compassion, but there was nobody;
for comfort, but could not find not a soul.

They put wormwood in my food,
and for my thirst gave me vinegar to drink.

May their table become a snare to contentment,
for their tranquility a trap.

May their eyes be covered by darkness, unable to see;
may their loins tremble and falter.

Pour out your wrath on them,
and let the kindling of your anger
overtake them as they run.

May their embattlements be laid waste by flood;
in their tents let there be none to dwell.

For you are the one who flattens pursuers to contrition.
Of those wounded while profaning your justice,
word quickly spreads.

The wage of wrongfulness impose on their wrongs;
keep them far from those who worship your ways.

Strike their names from the Book of Life;
with the virtuous do not mingle their mention.

O, I am troubled of spirit and sickened by grief.
Your salvation, my Upholder, will raise me to a place
    of rest.

I will praise you with words of my song,
exalt you by means of thanksgiving.

To you this will seem more pleasing
than the sacrifice of oxen with full horns.

The broken of spirit will see and rejoice.
Seekers of God—their hearts will be brought back
    to life.

Because the Holy One listens to the needy,
and the afflicted does not ignore.

Let the heavens and earth praise the Eternal,
the seas and all creatures in them.

Because the God of Justice will bring salvation to
      Zion,
and build for Judah cities where people peaceably
      dwell.
Those who were forced out will return.

And the seed of slaves will inherit it;
lovers of God's name will settle there.

Psalm 70
⊱━◆━○━◆━⊰

FOR THE CONDUCTOR OF THE ETERNAL SYMPHONY,
BY DAVID, A REMINDER.

God, remember to save me,
God, rush to my help.

May they be disgraced and humiliated,
those who seek an end to my life.

May they be fenced off from behind and disgraced,
those who take pleasure in my harm.

May they retreat in shame—
those who are so boastful in triumph.

May all who seek you rejoice and exult.

May they always say:
"Let God's presence be lifted high,
all lovers of your salvation."

As for me, I am afflicted and poor—
God, rush toward me!

You are my help and means of escape—
my Protector, do not come too late.

Psalm 71

In you, God, I have taken refuge.
Don't let me ever be made ashamed.

In your faithfulness, lift me up;
bring me relief.

Lean your ear toward me now;
respond to my cry of pleading.

Be for me a rock of strength
I can always come to.
You said you would save me.

Because you are my sheltering cliff,
my escape from pursuit,

Holy One, keep me from the hand
of those who intend harm,
from the hand of the wrongful and ruthless.

Because you are my hopefulness,
my Upholder, my Light,
the one who taught me trust from my youth.

Upon you I have relied from the womb;
from the uterus of my mother, you drew me out.

You have always been my object of praise.

I have been a sign of ruin to many,
but you were my shelter of strength.

Let my mouth flood over with worship!
All day long I will speak of your beauty.

Don't fling me away when I am old;
when my strength grows weak, don't forsake me.

For my enemies speak of me unkindly,
those who conspire to bring me down.
They say:

"God has abandoned him—

let us pursue and capture,
for there is none to bring respite."

My Shield—don't be distant.
My Sanctuary—rush to my help.

Let them be ashamed and overtaken,
those who threaten my life.

Let them be clothed in dishonor and scorn,
the ones who seek my destruction.

I will always wait for you.

I will heap praise on top of praise
until I can no longer remember their count;

my mouth will tell of your rightfulness,
your salvation all day long—

I will come with your might, my Upholder.

I will remember your faithfulness,
more powerful than anything else that exists.

God, you have taught me since my youth.
All this time, I have proclaimed your wonders
and will continue until old and gray.

Source of my Salvation, don't abandon me
until I proclaim your strength to this generation,
to all who come afterward, your steadfast presence.

Your rightfulness, God, reaches the highest of heavens,
you are the one who made every great expanse—

Eternal Life, who is like you?

You who have shown me so much affliction and trouble,
relent now and restore me to life.

From the ocean's depths,
return and raise me up.

Increase my sense of expanse;
turn around to bring me comfort.

I will spill out gratitude to you on the lute,
praise for your loyalty, my Upholder.

I will make melodies to you on the harp,
O Holy One of Israel.

My lips will sing out in joy;
I will compose for you melodies,
songs from the life you redeemed.

My tongue will murmur of your justice
all day long.

They will be ashamed and forever dishonored,
those who seek after my life.

Psalm 72

FOR SOLOMON.

Give insight of justice to the king,
wisdom to distinguish right from wrong to his son—

that he might judge your people fairly,
the poverty-stricken with vision of the just.

Let mountains lift up peace for the people
and the valleys flower with virtue.

May he bring justice to the poor,
hope to children who hunger,
crushing all the oppressors to dust.

Generation after generation will feel awe at your
    presence
in the sun's staggering brightness,
in the luminous blue of the moon.

May God descend—like rain sprinkled on grass after
    mowing,
like showers drenching the surface of the earth.

May the righteous king flower in his day,
with abundance of peace until the vanishing of the
    moon.

May results of his justice extend from sea to sea,
from the river to the ends of the earth.

Those who live in the desert will kneel before him.
His enemies will lick up dust.

Kings of Tarshish and the shorelands
will return with tribute of grain.

Kings of Sheva and Sava
will come with homage of drink.

All kings will bow down to him,
all nations serve him.

For the righteous king rescues the hopeless
when they cry for salvation,
the afflicted when there is none to bring help.

He shelters the downtrodden and weak,
and the lives of the impoverished he saves.

From the midst of violence
he redeems their life;
their blood is precious in his eyes.

The poor will live and give him gold of Sheva,
praying for his welfare constantly,
blessing him every day.

There will be a mantle of grain throughout the land,
even on peaks of mountains.

Leaves of the fruit trees will rustle like the great trees
    of Lebanon;
growth will sprout up in the city like grass in the field.

His name will last forever;
before the sun, his name will flourish.

And all who live will find blessing through him—
all nations praise his power.

The Holy One fills us with awe;
God of Israel,
the one who works wonders all alone.

May the holiness of your presence be praised,
the whole earth filled with your glory.

Amen and amen.
The praises of David, son of Jesse, are complete.

Psalm 73

A PSALM BY ASAF.

God is truly good to Israel,
truly good to the pure of heart.

As for me, my legs almost stumbled;
my feet almost slipped from underneath.

For I was envious of the arrogant;
only peace for the wrongful did I see.

Because there is no cord binding them to death;
their stomachs are always content.

They do not suffer the ordinary struggles of mortals;
they are not struck with affliction
like the rest of humankind.

Pride is the adornment around their neck.
Their clothing is a shawl of violence.

Their eyes bulge with greed.
They have exceeded the desire of their hearts.

They melt others with words of cruelty;
they speak as though on high.

They place their mouths in heaven,
but their tongues traverse the earth—

so God's people turn against what is holy,
and from a full cup squeeze only a drop.

They say: "What does the Eternal know?
Is there really knowledge in the heights?"

Behold these people, the wrongful—
they are continually content,
having attained great wealth.

And so, is it for this nothingness that I purified my
    heart?
That I washed my hands clean of stain?

To be struck with divine wrath all day,
punishment every morning when I wake?

If I were to tell what I have suffered,
behold! I would be a traitor to your children's
    generation.

And when I pondered this,
all life seemed trouble and turmoil in my eyes—

until I entered your holy sanctuaries,
and understood that even they come to an end.

You place them on slippery ground;
you level them to a wasteland.

How can destruction come so suddenly?

Everything comes to an end abruptly
and is finished by terrors
too frightening to recount—

like a dream that flings one awake.
God, in the midst of the city, ransack the enemy's
    image.

Because my heart has become like vinegar,
my mind thrust with torment.

I have been senseless and did not know.
I have been like an animal with you.

Yet I am always at your side.
You take hold of my right hand.

In your counsel, guide me.
Take me toward your holy presence.

Who is for me in the heavens?

When I am with you, I desire nothing else on earth.
What is left of myself and my heart are extinguished.

Rock of my Faith and my Portion:
your blessing of Life continues forever.

For behold—those far from you will vanish.

Put an end to my idolatrous straying.
Closeness to God is my only true good.

I have made you, the Holy One, my shelter,
that I might continually proclaim all your wonders.

Psalm 74

A PSALM IN SEARCH OF UNDERSTANDING, BY ASAF.

Why, God? Have you rejected us forever?
Will your anger smolder against the sheep that you
    graze?

Remember those who bear witness to you,
those who entered your covenant long ago,
those you redeemed to give testimony to your ways.

Remember Mount Zion—this place where you
    dwelled.
Will you raise your feet to wreak eternal ruin?

See the devastation the enemy has brought on your
    temple!
Destroyers rage in your meeting places.
They set up their emblems as signs from their god.

It was thought to have come from heaven.
In the thicket of trees—hatchets.

And now they have broken it open, splintering its
    engravings.
With axe and sledgehammer they have struck it down.

They set your sanctuary on fire,
profaning your name's dwelling place on earth.

They said in their hearts: "Let us destroy all their
    offspring.
Let us burn all the holy places in the land."

Our portents—we have not seen them.

A prophet no longer exists;
there is no one among us who knows how long.

Until when, God?
How long will the oppressor taunt us?
Will the enemy blaspheme your name forever?

Why do you restrain your hand,
keep your right arm to your breast?

You have been my source of direction from the
    beginning,
giving salvation throughout the land.

You, God—you shattered the sea with your strength,
smashing the heads of serpents upon the water.

You crushed the brain of Leviathan,
giving him as food to people,
carnage to wild beasts.

You split open springs and torrents.
You caused mighty rivers to grow dry.

Day belongs to you, also the night.
You taught the stars and sun where to shine.

You carved all the earth's boundaries;
summer and winter—you sculpted them.

Remember this:

a cruel enemy provoked you.
A corpse-like people insulted your name.

Don't relinquish your sweet dove to wild beasts.

The life of your afflicted—
don't let it escape your consideration forever.

Turn your eyes toward the covenant,
for the dark places of earth
are filled with dwellings of violence.

Don't let the discouraged cringe away hopeless.
The poor and hungry—they praise your name.

Rise up, God, contend your quarrels,
remember how you are degraded
by the coldhearted each day.

Don't forget the voices of those turned against you.
The roar of your contenders
continues to constantly rise.

Psalm 75

FOR THE CONDUCTOR OF THE ETERNAL SYMPHONY,
A PLEA TO BE SPARED DESTRUCTION, BY ASAF, A SONG.

We are thankful to you, God;
we are grateful; your name is always close to our lips.

Everyone speaks of your wonders.

You say:
For I will appoint a time
when I will judge with fairness and truth.

The earth may melt and all who dwell on it,
but I will sturdy its pillars—Selah.

I have said to the boastful:
Don't praise yourselves.

And to the unjust:
Don't raise toward heaven
your foolish horn of pride.
You speak with arrogant neck.

For not from the place where the sun rises
and not from twilight,
not from the wilderness are we lifted up.

The God of Justice judges.
One person is brought low and another is raised up.

A cup is in the hand of the Creator,
filled with a frothing wine, full of spices,
and from it, God pours.

The unjust of the land will find and drink only its
   remnants.

I will proclaim the Eternal wonders to the world,
make song to the Upholder of Jacob.

I will hack down the pride of the wrongful
but the strength of the righteous will continue to rise.

Psalm 76

FOR THE CONDUCTOR OF THE ETERNAL SYMPHONY,
ON MUSICAL INSTRUMENTS, A PSALM BY ASAF, A SONG.

God is well-known in Judah;
in Israel, reputation of the Creator is widespread.

And so will it be when your tabernacle of peace
is built in Jerusalem, your dwelling place in Zion.

There you shattered arrows that blazed fire bolts,
shield and sword and bloodshed—Selah.

You are filled with light, leaving us more humbled
than the sight of mountains of corpses.

The valiant of heart languish like spoil;
they drowse away their final hour.

And all the warriors, they cannot find their hands.

From your rebuke, God of Jacob,
chariot and horse are stunned into slumber.

You fill us with wonder—you!

Who can stand in your sight
when your divine wrath rages?

From the heavens you made heard your judgments.
The land was quiet with awe.

When you rise to judge humankind,
all the humble of the earth will be saved—Selah!

People will give thanks even in their anger.
The remnant of their rage you will restrain.

Make vows and fulfill them to the Eternal One, God;
all who are near, bring gifts to the source of wonder.

The Holy One cuts off breath
of those who oppose goodness,
filling all the earth's leaders with awe.

Psalm 77

For the Conductor of the Eternal Symphony,
to the Beloved, by Asaf, a psalm.

My voice lifts toward God and I cry out.
My voice lifts toward my Provider,
and you lean down to listen.

In times of affliction, I have sought your presence.
My hand reaches forth during the night without resting.
My soul refuses comfort.

I remember how it used to be, and I moan.
I try to speak but my soul gets tangled in knots—
     Selah.

Will my Upholder forsake me forever?
Will your favor never return?

Has your kindness been extinguished for all time?
Your eternal word vanished for all generations?

Have you forgotten how to give freely?
Has the drawstring of your compassion been forever
     closed?

I have said: Is it my fault
that the hand of God has changed against me?

I remember your works;
I recall your previous wonders.

I ponder your deeds,
I contemplate your acts.

God, your every path is holy.
What power is as vast as the Creator's?

You are the One who brings the world alive with
     wonder.
You make your strength known to all nations.

You restored your people with your right arm,
the children of Jacob and Joseph—Selah.

The water saw you, God, and writhed in anguish.
Even the depths trembled in fear.

The dark clouds streamed forth water.
The storm clouds gave forth voice.

The sound of your thunder was heard in the
      whirlwind—
lightning illumined the earth.
The world trembled and quaked.

Your pathway traverses the sea.
Wake of your presence can be seen in the wide
      waters—
and what comes as a consequence, nobody knows.

You have guided your people like a flock of sheep,
by the hand of Moses and Aaron.

Psalm 78

A SONG FOR UNDERSTANDING, BY ASAF.

Listen, my people, to my teaching,
bend down your ears to the utterance of my mouth.

I will open my mouth with a parable,
express my intent
with riddles from long ago,

words we heard and knew,
truths our ancestors once told in stories.

We will not conceal them from their children,
but rather declare to later generations

praises of God's strength,
wonders the Holy One has done.

The All-Knowing raised up a testimony for Jacob,
a teaching of holiness for Israel—

that which our ancestors were instructed
to convey to their offspring,

so that future generations would understand,
those still unborn.

They would arise and recount it to their children
so their children would put their trust in God,

and not forget divine wonders,
keeping close to the eternal will,

and not be like those who came before—
a stubborn and oblivious generation,

a generation that failed to direct its heart,
whose spirit held no faith.

The children of Ephraim kissed the enemy's
    bowstrings.
They turned weak on the day of battle.

They didn't keep the covenant,
refused to follow God's teaching.

They forgot about the Creator's acts,
the beauty and holiness that the Source of Life
    revealed.

God, in plain sight of our ancestors you performed
    wonders—
in the land of Egypt and the field of Tzoan.

You split the sea and shepherded them across.
You made the water stand as though amazed.

You guided them with a cloud by day,
all night with a blaze of fire.

You split rocks in the wilderness
and gave them water to drink,
as though it came from great depths of sea.

You brought forth streams from granite;
they gushed out like water from a mighty river.

But they continued to misunderstand you,
to rebel against the Sustainer during drought.

And they tested you in their hearts,
asking for bread beyond their need.

And they spoke, saying,
"Can God prepare a table in the wilderness?

True, the Source of Life struck a rock
and water flowed from streambeds—
it came forth in a flood;

but can the Transcendent One also provide bread?
Can you keep alive the remnant of the people?"

Then you heard and were torn apart.
A fire was kindled in Jacob, smoke rose up in Israel,
for they had no faith in the Upholder of Good.

They did not trust you would save them.
You commanded rain clouds above,
flinging open the doors of heaven.

You rained on them manna to eat,
and gave them the grain of heaven.

Each person was nourished and sated.
You hurled down venison until they could eat no more.

You caused the east wind to blow in heaven,
guided them with strength toward the south.

You rained upon them meat flesh like a dust storm;
you sent them winged fowl abundant as grains of sand.

It fell in the midst of their tents,
all around where they dwelt.
They ate until fully content.

Everything they craved you brought them.
They were no strangers to their desires.

Again and again, they found food in their mouths.
But your anger rose against them;
they were killed by their own greed—

until Israel's youth fell to their knees.

With all of this, they failed to see you
and had no faith in your wonders.

And so their days were spent in futility,
their years in utter terror.

When they were dying, they sought you;
they repented and prayed to their Upholder.

They remembered that the Holy One was their Rock,
the Highest of High their redeemer.

But they deceived you with their mouths,
with their lips lied outright.

Their hearts were not loyal;
they had no faith in the covenant.

But you are compassionate, forgiving wrong,
never causing destruction.

Again and again, you hold back anger,
never awakening the entirety of your rage.

You remember that they are flesh,
a body that walks the earth never to return.

How often they rebelled against you in the desert,
bringing you sorrow in Shimon.

They turned away, fleeing the Source of Life;
Holy One of Israel, they caused you pain.

They did not remember the work of your hand,
the day you rescued them from torment.

You placed signs in Egypt,
wonders in the field of Tzoan.

You turned their river to blood;
from its streambed the oppressors
no longer could drink.

You sent a swarm of stinging flies, which devoured
    them,
and frogs, which brought destruction.

You gave their crop to devouring insects,
their labor to locusts.

Their vine you truncated with hail,
their sycamore trees with frost.

You surrounded their cattle with lightning,
their livestock with bolts of fire.

You sent against them blazing wrath—
fury, outrage, anguish,
heavenly messengers of the evil they would face.

God, you level a path with your anger.

You did not prevent them from dying,
but ended their lives with plague.

You struck the firstborn of Egypt,
the most violent among the tents of Cham.

You led out your people like sheep,
shepherded them like a flock in the wilderness.

You led them to safety and they were not afraid;
their enemies were swallowed by sea.

You brought them to the place of your holiness.
The mountain, this one, that your right hand had won.

You pushed nations from before their path,
giving them the landscape of their inheritance.

You dwelt in their tents, the tents of Israel's tribes.

But they tested and rebelled against the Eternal,
    Most High.
Testimony of the Holy One—they did not keep it.

They backslid and betrayed, just like their parents.
They became a slack and useless bow.

They angered you with idolatrous altars,
provoked you with statues of false gods.

You heard and flowed with outrage,
relinquishing Israel completely,

abandoning the tabernacle of Shiloh,
the tent where you dwelled among humankind.

You let your strength be taken captive,
your emblem of beauty fall to hand of your foe.

You gave your people over to the sword;
anger flowed toward your own inheritance.

Your youth were devoured by fire,
your virgins no longer praised in song.

Your priests fell by the sword,
Your widows, they no longer cried.

Then you rose as though from sleep,
like a warrior emboldened with wine.

You struck down those who opposed you.
You sent them eternal disgrace.

You rejected the tent of Joseph.
The tribe of Ephraim, you no longer chose.

You picked the tribe of Judah,
mountain of Zion that you love;

you built a holy temple like the loftiest sky,
like the earth, a foundation forever.

You chose David to be your servant.

You took him from enclosures of sheep.
From the midst of nursing lambs, you brought him
    out

to shepherd Jacob, a holy people;
Israel, nation of your inheritance.

You shepherded them with simplicity of heart,
With your hands, you gave them good guidance.

Psalm 79

A PSALM, BY ASAF.

God, nations invade what belongs to you;
they profane your holy temple,
leaving Jerusalem a twisted heap of ruins.

They turn your servants into corpses,
food for birds of the sky;

the flesh of those who love you
has been given to brutes of the earth.

They pour out their blood like water
into the Jerusalem streets—

there is none left to even dig a grave.

We have been a disgrace to our neighbors,
a mockery and laughingstock to those all around.

How long, God?
Will you be furious with us forever?
Will your anger burn, as with fire?

Pour out your rage, instead,
on nations that don't know you,
kingdoms that don't call out your name.

For they have devoured Jacob,
laid waste his tranquil pastures.

Don't remember of us our earlier sins.
Come quickly with compassion,
for we have been brought very low.

Help us, God of our salvation,
to make known the glory of your name.

Rescue us; forgive our mistakes—
because that is your nature.

Why do the nations say,
"Where is their God?"

Let it be known among nations, seen by our eyes—
the payment for your servant's spilled blood.

Let the prisoner's groan come before you.
In keeping with the great strength of your arm,
keep alive those sentenced to death.

Return to our neighbors what they have done—
return it sevenfold upon their chests.
Disgrace them as they have disgraced you, my
    Upholder.

But we are your people, sheep that you graze.
We will thank you forever.

From generation to generation we will repeat all your
    praises.

Psalm 80

FOR THE CONDUCTOR OF THE ETERNAL SYMPHONY,
ON A LILY-SHAPED INSTRUMENT,
A TESTIMONY BY ASAF, A PSALM.

Shepherd of Israel, open your ear;
lead Joseph like a flock of sheep.

Holy One, enthroned by cherubim,
appear and shine brightly.

Before Ephraim, Benyamin, and Menasheh
awaken your strength; stride forth to our salvation.

Living God, cause us to return;
Light up your face and we will be saved.

Source of Hope, Creator of the Heavenly Array,
How long will your smoke kindle
against the prayer of your people?

You fed them bread of weeping,
made them drink their own tears
by the mouthful.

You have subjected us to strife among our neighbors;
our enemies hold us in scorn.

Creator of the Heavenly Array,
cause us to return to you.
Light up your face, and we will be saved.

You caused a vine to stretch forth from Egypt,
made a small garden among the nations and planted it.

You cleared space in the soil around it,
prepared a hole for its roots to grow.
Now it fills the earth.

The mountains were covered by its shadow.
Its branches became mighty cedars of God.

You caused its boughs to stretch toward the sea,
toward the river, its tender shoots.

Why have you broken through its fences,
leaving all who pass by to pluck its fruit?

The boar of the forest ravages it;
all that moves through the field
gnaws on its remains.

Creator of the Heavenly Array,
come back, I plead with you.

Gaze down from the sky and see.
Be mindful of this vine.

Take care of the root your right hand planted,
the children you strengthened in your service.

They burn in flame like human dung.
From the absence of your presence, they perish.

Place your hand over each person, your right arm
over every human life—strengthen them toward you.

Then we will not build fences from you, backing away.
Let us live; we will cry out your name.

Eternal Creator of the Heavenly Array,
turn toward us.

Light up your face
and we will be saved.

Psalm 81

For the Conductor of the Eternal Symphony,
upon the wine-press instrument, by Asaf.

Sing out to the Creator, source of our strength;
give a trumpet blast to the Upholder of Jacob.

Lift your voice in song; beat on your drum,
play melodies on the harp along with the lyre.

Blast a shofar during the new moon,
which covers with dark our time of rejoicing.

For it is a statute for Israel,
eternal law by the Upholder of Jacob—

who placed it as testimony before Joseph
when he went down into Egypt's land:
"I heard a language I did not know."

I removed the burden from his shoulder.
His hands were lifted from their weight.

In constriction you called out, and I pulled you from
    harm.
I will answer you now from the place of hidden thunder.

I tested you at the Waters of Contention—Selah.

Listen, my people, and I will defend you—
Israel—if you would only hear to my voice.

Let there be no strange god among you;
do not bow down to a power you have never known.

I am God, your Source of Life,
the one who brought you up from the land of Egypt.
Open your mouth wide and I will fill it.

My people did not pay attention;
Israel did not want me.

I let them go forth in the hardness of their hearts.
They continued to follow their own counsel.

If only my people would listen to me,
if only Israel would walk in my ways.

In a short while I would humble their foes;
upon their oppressors I would lay my hand.

Those who reject God are dishonest,
but the Eternal waits for them forever,
saying:

I would feed you with the richest wheat;
from a rock, I would fill you with honey.

Psalm 82

A PSALM OF ASAF.

God, you stand amidst all the flawed objects of praise;
from among the false gods you will judge.

How long, God, will you tolerate injustice,
lifting the spirits of those who refuse to do right?—
   Selah.

Bring justice to the downtrodden and orphaned.
The poor and the hungry, protect their rights.

Rescue the needy and afflicted;
from the hands of the wrongful, lift them away.

They don't know and don't understand—
in darkness they pace back and forth.

Foundations of the earth all violently tremble.

I have said to humanity—you are made in the image
   of God,
handiwork of the Most High, all of you.

But like mortals you will die;
like royalty you will tumble.

Rise up, God, judge the earth,
for all nations belong to you.

Psalm 83

A SONG, A PSALM OF ASAF.

God, don't stifle yourself from speaking;
don't deafen yourself to my plea;
don't stiffen into silence, Spark of my Strength.

For look! Your enemies whisper against you;
those who hate you raise up their heads.

Against your people they scheme in secret.
They conspire against your treasure.

They say—"Let us go and erase their nation.
The name of Israel will be remembered no more."

They join forces with one heart;
against you, they make an alliance.

The tents of Edom and Ishmael,
Moav and those of Hagar.

Gavel and Amnon and Amalek,
Philistine and the settlers of Tyre.

Ashur, too, went along with them.
They were a right arm to the children of Lot—Selah.

Do to them as you did to Midyan,
to Sisera and Yavin at the waters of Kishon.

They were destroyed at the Wellspring of Dor.
Their corpses were compost for earth.

Make their nobles like Orev, the Raven,
and Zev, the Wolf,

all the princes like Zevach, the Sacrifice,
all their molten idols
like Tzalzuma, the Shadow of Withholding—

all those who boasted they would dispossess us
from the pleasant pastures of God.

My Upholder—make them like a whirlwind,
like dry grass before a breeze.

Be like a fire that blazes through a forest,
a ravenous flame that sears a mountain pass.

Like that, pursue them with your storm;
with your tempest, humble them into terror.

Fill their faces with dishonor
until they seek out your Holy Name.

Without your presence before them,
they will always be terrified and ashamed,
lonely and lost.

Then they will know that you—
your name alone is God.
You—most worthy of praise over all the earth.

Psalm 84

FOR THE CONDUCTOR OF THE ETERNAL SYMPHONY,
ON THE WINE FESTIVAL LYRE,
BY THE OFFSPRING OF KORACH, A PSALM.

How beloved are the places we perceive you,
Arranger of the Heavenly Spheres.

My soul pales with languish,
longing for your courtyards—

my heart and my flesh
cry out to the Source of Life.

Even the bird finds a home,
the wild swallow a nest for her young;
she offers her fledglings upon your altars.

Creator of the stars and planets,
my Earthly Protector and my Heavenly God,

happy are the ones who dwell in your house.
Again and again they will praise you—Selah.

Content are the ones whose strength comes from you;
their heart is an easy road.

Those who cross through the Valley of Weeping
transform it into a wellspring of life.

Your rain covers them with blessings.
They walk from strength to strength
witnessed by God in Zion.

Living Presence, Arranger of the Heavenly Spheres,
listen intimately to my prayer.

Open your ear, Upholder of Jacob, Selah.
Our Shield—look, God—
gaze on the face of the one anointed by your grace.

Because a day in your courtyards
is sweeter than a thousand somewhere else.

I would rather stand on the threshold,
the threshold of your house,
than dwell in the tents of those estranged from your
    will.

For a sun and a shield is God, Sustainer of All
    Creation.
The love and honor we crave—the Source of
    Abundance will give it to us.

God refuses no goodness to all who walk the holy
    road.

Arranger of the Heavenly Spheres,
happy is the one who trusts completely in you.

Psalm 85

FOR THE CONDUCTOR OF THE ETERNAL SYMPHONY,
BY THE OFFSPRING OF KORACH, A PSALM.

You longed for your land, God.
You returned Jacob to its borders.

You lifted away the distortions of your people.
You covered their many mistakes—Selah.

You contained the flood of your anger.
You turned back from the heat of your wrath.

Turn back to us now, God of salvation.
Break off from us your rage.

Will you be angry with us forever?
Will you continue in your fury
from one generation to the next?

If only you would restore us to life,
your people would rejoice in you.

Show us, God, your kindness,
and your salvation—give us your help.

I will listen to your will,
Foundation of my Strength.

For you speak peace to your people
and will not let the faithful engage in futility.

Rather your uplift is close
to those who hold you in awe—
glory will once again dwell in our land.

Kindness and truth will meet each other—
justice and tranquility kiss.

Truth will sprout up from the earth,
love for humanity look down from the sky,

God will once again grant plenty,
and our land will yield a good crop.

Righteousness will walk before us,
placing feet of the faithful on the right road.

Psalm 86

A PRAYER, BY DAVID.

Lean your ear close, God, respond to my cry,
for I am poor and desperate.

Watch over my soul,
for I am among those who love you.

Save your servant—you are my Protector!—
and I, the one who trusts in your care.

Draw toward me with compassion, my Sustainer,
for it is to you I cry out all day.

The soul of your servant is made glad,
because to you, my Upholder, I lift it up.

For you are kind and forgiving,
full of love to all who call out in pain.

Turn your ear, God, to my prayer;
Pay attention to the sound of my pleading.

When I am in trouble, I call out to you,
for you always respond.

The false gods do not even approach you, my Creator.
Nothing compares to your deeds.

All nations that you have created, God,
will come and bow before you,
giving honor to the glory of your name.

For you are present everywhere, performing wonders.
You alone are Infinite.

Teach me, my Protector, your path
and I will walk in your truth.

Piece together my heart
to be wondrous of your name.

I will thank you, my God,
my Upholder, with all my heart.
I will forever glory in your ways.

For your love is spread vast upon me;
you lifted my soul from depths of despair.

God—the arrogant rise against me.
Those who use terror
seek to destroy my life.

They have not placed your presence before them.

But you, my Upholder,
are a God of compassion, giving freely,
slow to anger, endless in love and truth.

Turn toward me; reply to my cry for compassion.
Give to your servant from your wellspring of
    strength.

Save the offspring of those faithful to your will.

Make me an emblem of goodness
so that my haters will look
and turn back ashamed.

For you are God;
you have helped and consoled me.

Psalm 87

>─◆─○─◆─◄

BY THE OFFSPRING OF KORACH, A PSALM,
  A SONG,
WITH FOUNDATION ON THE HOLY MOUNTAINS.

God loves the gates of Zion
more than all the dwellings of Jacob.

Words of glory are spoken about it,
city of the Living God—Selah.

I need only mention Rahav and Babylonia to those
    I know.
Look! there is a man from Philistine and Tyre,
along with another from Kush;
one of them was born there.

Of Zion it is said,
everyone was born in its borders.
And God who is Most High made it firm.

The Creator will count them
when writing nations into the Book of Life:

this one was born there—Selah,

poets as well as profaners—
all my wellsprings come from you.

Psalm 88

A SONG, A MELODY
BY THE OFFSPRING OF KORACH,
FOR THE CONDUCTOR OF THE ETERNAL SYMPHONY
AT A TIME OF ILLNESS, PLEADING FOR ANSWERS,
A SONG IN SEARCH OF UNDERSTANDING,
BY HEMAN THE EZRACHITE.

Eternal One, Source of my Salvation,
by day I cried out to you for help;
I tried to approach you each night.

Let my prayer come before you now;
lean down your ears to my cry.

For my soul is filled with torment.
My life is like the walking dead.

I have been thought of as one
who has gone down to the pit,
one without even strength to protest.

Among the dead I am free,
like the anonymous slain who lie in the grave,
those you remember no more,
because they were cut off from life by your hand.

You have thrown me down into a well of despair,
into dark shadows of the thickest depths.

Your wrath pressed down against me,
all your crashing waves of affliction—Selah.

My acquaintances—they have all grown estranged.
You made me loathsome to them.

From my confinement, I cannot struggle free.
My eyes are weak from hunger.

I call out to you, God, every day.
I spread my palms before you in prayer.

Is it for the dead you work wonders?
If the healed rise, they will thank you—Selah.

Is your kindness spoken of in the grave?
Your loyalty praised among those lost from the living?

Are your wonders known in darkness?
Your justice in the land of oblivion?

And I—it is to you, my Upholder, that I have cried
     for help.
Each morning I come before you in prayer.

Why, God, have you abandoned my life
and hidden your face from me?

I have been afflicted and dying since youth.
I have carried terror of you and confusion.

Across my flesh has flashed your burning anger.
Fear of you has withered my life.

My nightmares surround me like water.
They gather around like a single voice.

You have pushed away from me both friend and
    lover.
All my acquaintances have vanished in the dark.

Psalm 89

A SONG FOR UNDERSTANDING, BY EITAN THE
    EZRACHITE.

God, your love lasts forever;
I will sing of you to each generation,
make known through my mouth your faithful
    presence.

For I have said: The world is built through kindness.
The heavens—you arranged them with your care.

I established a covenant with my chosen one,
made an oath to David, my servant,

that I would sustain your children forever,
that in each generation
I would uphold your throne—Selah.

The heavens proclaim your wonders, God—
your faith is known wherever the holy ones gather.

For who in the clouds compares to the Creator;
who among false gods
resembles image of the Most High?

The mystics tremble at your strength.
Those all around are awed by your power.

Creator of the Heavenly Array, who is strong like you?
Your faithfulness shines all around.

You rule the prideful sea.
When the waves rise up, you soothe them.

You crush the arrogant to dust.
With your mighty arm you scatter all who oppose
    you.

The heavens belong to you as well as the earth,
inhabited land and all it contains.
You are their foundation.

North and east—you created the compass.
Tabor and Hermon, they sing with joy at your name.
To you belong power and might.

Your hand strengthens us;
your right arm is raised.

Faith and justice are your throne's foundation.
Kindness and truth precede your presence.

Happy are those who know the sound of the shofar.
They walk, my Upholder, in the light of your face.

They rejoice in your name all day long.
They exult at your justice.

For you are the beauty that underlies our strength.
Through your will, you give us new vigor.

For our shield is the Eternal;
to the Holy One of Israel we give allegiance.

Then you spoke in a vision to your faithful, saying:

My help came through a man of conviction;
I raised up a youth from among the people.

I found David, my servant,
and anointed him with my holy oil—

so that my hand was with his hand;
my muscle gave him strength.

No enemy will rise up against him;
no force of injustice will cause him harm.

I will beat down all his sources of anguish;
his despisers—I will push them away.

My faithfulness and kindness are with him;
and when he calls upon me,
so is my strength.

I will place his left hand on the ocean,
his right on the river.

He will call to me—"You are my Upholder,
My God and Rock of my Salvation."

I will make him my firstborn,
more exalted than any other ruler of the earth.

I will keep my love for him forever;
my covenant will be worthy of trust.

I will uphold his offspring always;
his throne will be long as the days of heaven.

If his children forsake my teaching,
refusing to walk in my justice,

if they profane my eternal statutes,
scorning what is right,

then I will respond to their rebellion
with a staff of reproach,
trouble with plagues their turning away.

But my kindness I will never reclaim,
never prove false to my faithfulness.

I will not profane my agreement;
what issues from my lips I will never change.

One thing I swore in my holiness,
that I would never betray David for all time.

His seed will endure forever,
his throne like the sun before my eyes.

Like the moon, it will remain steadfast forever,
a faithful witness in the sky—Selah.

But you, God, have forsaken and rejected.
You have betrayed your anointed one,
our great and only hope.

You spurned the covenant with your servant,
let his crown be flung to the earth.

You broke through all his fences,
turned his strongholds into places of fear,

All who pass by plunder him.
He has become a disgrace to his neighbors.

You raised the right arm of his oppressors;
you made all his enemies rejoice.

You turned his sword to blunt rock,
refusing to uphold him during battle.

You put an end to his purity,
knocked his throne to the ground.

You shortened the days of his youth,
clothing him in shame—Selah.

How long, God? Will you remain hidden forever?
Your fury rages like a thirsty flame.

I ponder the length of a life span.
For what futility have you created humankind?

Who is the one who lives and never sees dying?
Who will never see his soul
slip to the underworld's grasp?—Selah.

Where are your earlier acts of love, my Upholder?
The ones you swore to David in your faithfulness?

Remember, God, the disgrace of your servant.
I have carried the contempt of many inside my chest.

Those who taunt us are your enemies, God!
They scorn the footsteps of your anointed.
Blessed is the Eternal forever. Amen and amen.

Psalm 90

A PRAYER OF MOSES, MAN OF GOD.

God, you have been a dwelling place for us
from one generation to the next.

Before mountains were born,
before earth and its people came to exist.

From eternity until eternity you are holy.

Mortals can turn to you until they are crushed.
You say, "Return, children of Adam."

Because a thousand years you can hold in your sight
like a yesterday passing into today,
a watchman's hour of relief at night.

You flood the years; they pass like sleep.
By morning, they vanish like grass.

At dawn a person flowers and is fragrant;
by evening we are withered and dry.

For by your wrath we are extinguished.
By your anger we are made to feel afraid.

You have laid out our transgressions before you,
our secrets are illumined by the light of your face.

All our hours pass by in your fury.
Our years come to an end as though imagined.

The years of our days are seventy;
if we are strong, maybe eighty.

All our boasts are toil and delusion,
because life passes and rushes and flies away.

Who can bear the force of your rejection?
Our fear of you seems to us like your anger.

Make known to us the portion of our days,
so we may gain a heart of wisdom.

Turn back to us, God—oh, how long?
Have compassion on those trying to serve your will.

Fill our morning with acts of your kindness
and we will sing and rejoice all our days.

Bring us joy in proportion to our days of affliction,
years we saw only strife.

May your acts be visible to your servants,
your splendor to their children's eyes.

May the sweetness of the Holy One, our Creator,
be constantly before us.

And the work of our hands, give us direction.
And the work of our hands—give it direction toward
   you.

Psalm 91

The one who dwells in the shelter of the Most High
sleeps in the shadow of God's breast.

I name the Eternal my refuge and fortress;
my God in whom I place my trust.

Because the Holy One will deliver you from the
   archer's trap,
from a plague that plows a swath of destruction.

Under sheltering wings, the Creator will protect you
    from sun.
Under feathers, the Protector will wrap you with
    refuge.

A shield and armor is God's truth.

So have no fear of the vague terror that comes at
    night,
the sharp arrow that flies by day.

Do not shudder at the plague that prowls by deepest
    dark,
the contagion that flattens by full-blown noon.

A thousand will fall at your left side,
a multitude will fall at your right,
but you it never will touch.

Only with your eyes will you behold suffering,
retribution for those who cause harm.

Because God is my refuge,
my dwelling place in the heights.

You will encounter no sorrow.
No plague will come near your tent

The Holy One will command angels
to guard you on all your paths.

On their hands they will carry you
lest you hurt your foot on a rock.

Upon lions and cobras you will walk safely;
serpents and young lions you will trample down.

Because you cling to me in love, says God,
I will carry you safely away.

I will lift you up, for you know my name.
When you call out to me, I will answer;

I am with you in times of affliction.
I will release you from harm
and illumine your honor.

I will satisfy you with long life
and show you the fruit of my salvation.

Psalm 92

A PSALM, A SONG FOR THE DAY OF SHABBAT.

It is good to be thankful to God,
to sing praises to your name, Most High,

to proclaim your kindness in the morning,
your faithfulness throughout the night,

upon the ten-stringed instrument and the lute,
upon soft voice accompanied by harp.

Because you have brought me rejoicing, God, with
    your acts;
upon witnessing your hands' creation, I cry out in
    awe.

How vast are your works, God.
Your thoughts are deep as a valley.

A woman with dull heart cannot know this;
a man with blunt intellect cannot understand.

When the wrongful sprout up like grass
and the workers of injustice blossom,
they will be destroyed by testimony of time.

But you remain in the heights forever.

For behold your enemies, God;
for behold, your enemies will be lost.

All the wrongful will be divided within.

You lift up my strength like a wild ox.
I glisten with sweet oil.

My eyes have seen those who watch for my fall.
When those who wish me harm rise up against me,
my ears have heard.

The righteous will spread their leaves like a palm tree;
like a cedar of Lebanon they will reach up high.

Planted in the house of God,
in the courtyards of our Creator,
they will give forth fruit.

They will continue to flower in old age,
their fruit will be ripe and fragrant—

to give testimony that God is clear in judgment,
my Rock in whom no flaw exists.

Psalm 93

God reigns, adorned with splendor.
Adorned with power, the Eternal is crowned with
    strength.

You made the earth firm so it would not falter.

Your throne is always steady.
You have been present from the beginning of time.

The rivers grew swollen, God.
They lifted their voice.
They raised their crashing waves.

More powerful than the roar of many waters,
mightier than the breaking sea,
invincible in the heights is your presence.

Your testimonies are faithful beyond measure.
Your house shines with holy splendor.

You live on, God, for the length of days.

Psalm 94

God who upholds the righteous—
God who upholds the righteous, shine out!

Lift yourself up, judge of all the earth.
Return to the boasting what they justly deserve.

How much longer, God,
how much longer will the wrongful exult?

Their mouths gush; they speak with arrogant tongues.
They talk with smugness, all who strive to bring
    sorrow.

Your people, God, have been crushed;
they have made your portion suffer.

The widow and stranger are slain;
helpless orphans lie slaughtered.

And they said: "God will not see.
The Upholder of Jacob will not notice their plight."

Understand now, you brutish ones.
You who are ignorant—how much longer will you fail
   to comprehend?

The One who shapes the ear, does the Listener not
   hear?
The One who creates the eye, does the All-Knowing
   not see?

The One who restrains nations, does the Creator not
   rebuke them?
The One who teaches humanity to reason?

You know the thoughts of humankind,
how they are futile and fleeting.

Happy is the one whom you restrain.
From your teaching, you give us instruction—

to quiet us during turmoil
until a pit is dug for the oppressors.

For you will not abandon your people.
You will not forsake those who choose the holy as
   their own.

The courts will once again become righteous,
the wise-hearted will walk in their light.

Who will rise to my defense against the wrongful?
Who will stand for me against those who strive to
   bring harm?

If only God would help—
My soul dwells almost in silence.

When I try to speak, my legs give way beneath.
Only your kindness, my Source of Hope, holds me
    upright.

When a tangle of anxiety troubles my chest,
your comfort revives my soul.

Have you made friends with the throne of
    destruction?
Has the creator of suffering engraved against me
    a law?

Wrongdoers leap upon the righteous.
They wound innocent blood.

But you will be a refuge for me;
a rock where I hide from destruction.

The strength of their corruption will come back to
    their chests.

Let their own wrong annihilate them;
let it overthrow their destruction,
Holy One, our God.

Psalm 95

Come, let us sing out to God!
Let us shout with joy to our Rock of Salvation!

Let us come before our Redeemer with thanks,
proclaim with music the Holy Name.

For you are a far-reaching power,
towering sovereign above all false objects of praise.

The one whose hand holds unexplored valleys;
peaks of great mountains are known to you alone.

The one to whom the sea belongs—it is you who
    made it.
And the dry land, your hands gave it shape.

Come, let us bow down and humble ourselves.
Let us praise the Holy One, our Maker.

For you are our Source of Strength,
and we, the people, the flock that you graze.

Today—if only they would listen to your voice:

Don't harden your heart, as at Merivah, the Place
    of Contention,
like the day you tested me in the desert,
when your ancestors put me on trial
though they had witnessed my work.

Forty years I remained estranged from that
    generation.
I said: These are a people of wandering heart.
They don't know my ways.

But even in my anger I promised:
If only they would come to my place of rest . . .

Psalm 96

Sing out to God a new song,
sing out to God, all the earth.

Sing out to the Source of Life, praise the Infinite
    Name,
proclaim from day to day
the Holy Presence in our lives.

Speak of God's glory to the nations,
to all people of divine wonders.

For you are vast and exalted beyond measure—
awe of you transcends
all false objects of praise.

Flawed beliefs of nations ultimately falter,
but the heavens were made
by the Upholder of Life.

A dignity and splendor precede you.
Strength and beauty dwell in your house.

Give allegiance to God, families of nations.
Give allegiance to God for glory and strength.

Give allegiance to God—glory is the Infinite Name.
Raise up an offering and enter the holy courtyards.

Bow down before the Eternal, before the heavenly
    splendor;
dance wildly before the Creator, all the earth.

Proclaim among nations: the Holy One reigns on high
    forever—
the one who firmed the earth's axis so it would not
    falter,
the one who judges nations with straightforward
    truth.

Let the heavens rejoice and the earth exult!
Let the sea thunder along with all that fills it!
Let the fields glory along with all they contain!

Then all trees of the forest will sing out with joy—
before God, for you are coming,
coming to judge the earth.

You will judge all people of the world justly,
all nations with steadfast truth.

Psalm 97

God orders the world, let the earth rejoice.
Let islands and coastlines cry out with joy.

Cloud and impenetrable darkness surround you,
righteousness and justice uphold your holy throne.

A fire breathes forth before you,
blazing all who scorn your will.

You illumine with lightning the world's surface.
When the earth sees it, it trembles.

Mountains melt like wax before the Holy One,
before the Foundation of all that exists.

The sky proclaims your righteousness,
all nations witness your glory.

Sculptors of greed will be overtaken by shame,
those who pride themselves in constructing false gods.

Bow down before your Creator,
all who uphold empty goals.

Zion will hear of it and rejoice.
The daughters of Judah will exult—

at your judgments, God, for you are holy,
Highest Presence over all the earth.

Your truth is lifted beyond all falsity.
Those who love their Upholder oppose everything
    unkind.

You guard the souls of the faithful—
from the wrongdoer's hand, you lift them away.

A light is sown for the righteous,
eternal joy for the steadfast of heart.

Rejoice, O righteous, in God.
Give thanks for remembrance of the holy.

Psalm 98

A PSALM.

Sing out to God a new song—
for all the wonders of creation.

Salvation is in your right hand,
your arm emanates with the holy.

You announced your presence
before the nations,
revealing the extent of your justice.

You made your love and devotion known
to the house of Israel.

All reaches of the earth saw your salvation.

Shout out to God, all the earth!
Break forth into joy and melody!

Make music to the Eternal with a harp;
with a harp and a voice filled with song.

With trumpets and voice of the shofar
cry out before our Provider, the Spark of our
    Life.

Let the sea thunder along with all that fills it,
the earth and all who dwell on its land.

Rivers will clap their hands,
rejoicing along with the mountains—

before the face of God,
for you are coming,
coming to judge the earth.

You will judge all people of the world justly,
all nations with steadfast truth.

Psalm 99

God, you rule forever; nations quake.
Enthroned among cherubim—the earth shivers.

Your greatness is manifest in Zion,
your presence exalted in every nation.

They give thanks to your name—
for it is vast, awe-inspiring, and holy.

The strongest ruler is the lover of justice.

You uphold fairness,
acting with virtue and justice to Jacob.

Exalt the Eternal, our God, in praise,
bow down before the footstool
of the holy throne.

This Moses and Aaron did in their priesthood,
and Samuel, when he called out your name.

They called out to the All-Powerful
and were answered—

through a pillar of cloud, you spoke.
They kept to the eternal testimony,
and you gave them immortal law.

Holy One, our God, you answered.
You became for them a God of forgiveness,
admonishing them when they wandered astray.

Exalt the Eternal, our God, in praise;
bow down before the holy mountain.

For God, our God, is holy.

Psalm 100

A PSALM OF THANKSGIVING.

Shout out with joy, all who live on earth.
Serve the Holy One with rejoicing.

Come before the Upholder with a ringing cry.
Know that God is a source of wonder.

You created us, and it is to our Creator we belong.
We are shepherded by heavenly guidance.

Come into the divine gates with thankfulness,
the holy courtyards shining with praise.

Be thankful, awed by the Holy Name.
For God is good;

your kindness is toward the world.
From generation to generation, you remain faithful.

Psalm 101

By David, a psalm.

Of kindness and justice, I sing.
To you, O Holy One, I make melodies.

I study the path of simplicity.
How long until you come to me?

I have lived in my house with a clear heart,
have not placed before my eyes
things of no worth.

Those who swerve from you—
I have stayed from them distant.

None of it clings to me.
A twisted heart—I have turned from it away.
Evil—I do not study its path.

Those who speak slander of their neighbor in secret,
I will humble into silence.

The haughty eye and unsatisfied heart—
they are unable to know you.

My eyes are upon the world's faithful,
so they might dwell at my side.

Those who walk the path of simplicity
will be my help;

those who profess faith while acting unjustly,
they do not dwell in my house;

those who speak deceit
do not remain before my eyes.

Every morning, in my mind,
I wipe the wicked from the earth,

imagining a day
when all who bring sorrow
will vanish from the city of God.

Psalm 102

A PRAYER BY THE AFFLICTED UPON BEING OVERCOME BY
   WEAKNESS,
WHO POURS BEFORE GOD A COMPLAINT.

Listen, God, to my prayer;
my cry goes out to you alone.

Don't hide your face
on the day of my anguish.

Lean your ear toward me;
when I cry out, answer me quickly—

for my days are consumed like smoke;
my bones scorched like kindling.

Like grass struck by sun, my heart is withered.
I have forgotten how to eat my bread,

From sound of my moaning,
my bones cling to my flesh.

I am like a raven in the desert—
an owl estranged in desolate places.

I lie awake
like a lonely bird on the rooftop.

All day long my enemies provoke me;
those who scorn me speak of me falsely.

I have eaten ashes like bread.
My drink is mingled with weeping
because of your anger and rage—

for you lifted me up,
then flung me down.

My days are stretched like shadow.
And I, like grass, have grown withered and dry.

But you, God, are enthroned forever.
Memory of you continues from one generation
     to the next.

You! Rise up, take compassion on Zion.
For the time of relenting has come,
a time of rejoicing.

Those who serve you have cared for its stones,
yearned for even its dust.

Nations will stand in awe of your name,
all kings of the earth will know your glory.

For when you build Zion,
the holy presence will be revealed.

Turn toward the plea
of those whose heart is a wasteland;
don't reject their prayer.

Let this be written down for future generations,
so that people still unborn will offer praise.

For you gaze down from your heavenly abode,
looking from the sky toward earth—

to hear the groan of the prisoner,
to free those sentenced to death;

to proclaim the Holy Name in Zion,
praise the Eternal in Jerusalem

whenever people gather,
whenever kingdoms come together
to work in service of God.

My strength has been afflicted along the road;
my days grow short.

I say: My God! Do not lift me from my body
halfway through my life.

For your years continue from generation to
    generation.

You created the earth's foundation long ago.
And the heavens are craft of your hands.

They may vanish, but you will endure.

All of them like a garment will become tattered and
    worn.
Like a cloak you will change them;
they will fade away.

But you are different.
Your years never end.

You will see children of those who love you
settle in peace,
their seed established before your face.

Psalm 103

By David.

Be wild, O my soul, for the Source of Wonder;
let all my insides praise the Holy Name.

Be wild, O my soul, for the Source of Wonder;
don't let me forget all your kindness and help.

The one who forgives all my wrongs,
who heals me from sickness,
who rescues my life from the abyss—

who wraps me around with love and devotion,
who satiates my mouth with delight,
renewing my youth like an eagle's.

You make harmony,
bringing justice to all the oppressed.

You made your ways known to Moses,
your works to all the children of Israel.

You are compassionate, generous beyond limit,
quieting anger, abounding in love.

You do not hold on to a quarrel forever,
will not remember our faults for all time.

You do not requite us according to our errors,
do not demand from us in proportion to our wrongs.

For just as heavens tower above the earth,
so is your love upon those who hold you in awe.

Just as the eastern horizon is far removed from the
     west,
so does the Creator distance us from transgression.

Just as a mother has compassion for her child,
so do you have compassion
for those who hold you in awe.

For you know our inclinations
and remember that we are dust.

Mortals—our days are like grass.
Like a field that sprouts up, so do we blossom.

Like a wind that passes over the plant until it weakens
     and is gone,
so is the place where we stood remembered no longer.

But your love lasts from eternity until eternity,
settling upon those who hold you in awe.

Your righteousness continues toward our children's
     children,
to those who uphold your covenant with love;

those who remember your attention to our suffering
in order to learn from your acts.

You established a throne in the sky;
your guidance can be found everywhere we look.

Let the angels bless the Source of Life,
the mighty fulfill the heavenly word;
let them listen to the message of your tongue.

Let all the heavenly array praise you,
holy servants performing your will.

Let all creation praise you,
each plot of land declare your providence.

Be wild, O my soul, for the Source of Wonder.

Psalm 104

Stand in wonder, O my soul, before the Eternal.
Holy One, my God, you are vast beyond measure.

You are clothed in majesty and splendor,
wrapped in light as with a garment.

You stretch out the sky like a cloth,
rafters over water in the realms above.

You make clouds your chariot,
moving on wings of breathing air.

You makes winds your messengers,
blazing fire into the agent of your will.

You have steadied the earth on its foundation.
It will not collapse for all time.

The depths—you covered them as though with
    clothing.
Water stands in awe upon the hills.

It flees from your rebuke.
From the voice of your thunder, it trembles.

The mountains rise up, the valleys split open
to the very place you prepared.

You established a boundary that water cannot
    transgress.
It will not return again to cover the earth.

You send forth springs into rivers.
They flow between mountains;
you provide water to all beasts of the field.

With it, the wild ass quenches its thirst.
Upon the lake, the bird of heaven makes its home.
From amidst the bulrushes, it sends forth its voice.

You water the mountains from above.
From the fruit of your acts, the earth is sated.

You cause grass to sprout up for the cattle,
crops for the labor of human hands,

bringing forth bread from the earth,
wine to delight the human heart—

to make their faces glisten with oil,
and wheat, by which the human heart gains strength.

The trees of the Holy One are healthy and strong,
cedars of Lebanon that you planted.

In them, swallows build their nest;
the stork makes its home in the cypress.

The blustery mountains are made for the goat,
protecting cliffs for the badger.

You created the moon for festivals.
The sun—you know the place from where it came.

You placed down darkness, and there was night.
In it crawl all the beasts of the forest.

The young lions roar to tear limbs from their prey,
seeking their food from you.

The sun rises over the horizon and they crawl into
    hiding,
crouching down in their caves.

A person goes forth to labor,
to work until evening.

How vast are your works, God,
all of them created with wisdom.
Your craftsmanship overflows the world.

Behold! The sea—its distance is huge and wide.
In it, creatures crawl beyond number,
small fish along with the large.

There, ships lunge forth on the water.
Leviathan—you formed it to bask in the ocean.

All of them look toward you
to give them food in its time.

You provide it to them—they harvest it.
You open your hand and they eat their share of good.

You hide your face, and they are confounded,
    confused.
You take back their breath and they grow weak,
returning to the dust from which they were made.

You send forth your breath and they are created.
You renew the face of the earth.

Your glory continues forever;
may you always rejoice in your works!

The one who gazes toward earth and it trembles,
you touch the mountains and they smoke.

I will sing out to God with my life,
make melodies to the Creator with all my strength.

I will sweeten my conversation for your sake,
take joy in the Heavenly Upholder!

Soon sinners will vanish from the earth,
the wrongful exist no more.

Stand in wonder, O my soul, before the Eternal.
Let my soul shine praises on God.

Psalm 105

Pour out your thanks to God, call out the heavenly
    name.
Make known to the world the Provider's constant
    occasions.

Sing out to the Creator, make melodies,
speak of far-reaching wonders.

Brighten your heart with the Holy Name.
Be joyful, all who seek the Eternal Presence.

Search for divine strength.
Seek God's face always.

Recall the wonders our Creator has done,
omens and judgments
that flow from the heavenly mouth—

seed of Abraham, God's servant;
children of Jacob, the chosen ones.

You are eternal, our God.
Your justice can be found throughout the earth.

You remember your covenant forever;
the word you decreed
remains for a thousand generations,

the relation you engraved with Abraham,
your unbreakable oath to Isaac.

You made it stand immutable for Jacob,
for Israel as eternal accord,

saying, *To you I will give the promised land,*
pledge that you will have a portion.

This was a time when they were few in number,
a tiny presence wherever they dwelled.

They walked about from nation to nation,
from one kingdom to a people somewhere else.

You did not let those who oppress them rest,
rebuking royalty on their account.

Don't touch my anointed ones
and to my prophets do no harm.

You warned them of a famine in the land.
Every loaf of bread you broke in half.

You sent before them a man—
Joseph, sold as a slave.

They afflicted his feet with fetters;
iron shackled his soul—

until the Holy One arrived;
God's voice smelted his chains.

The king sent for Joseph and released him;
the ruler of people set him free.

Pharaoh made him a lord in his house,
controlling all its possessions,

with power to imprison princes when they threatened
    him,
insight to make his elders wise.

Then Israel came to Egypt;
Jacob came to dwell in the land of Cham.

You caused the people to bear fruit in abundance,
made them stronger than their enslavers.

But Egypt's heart turned to despise your nation,
to plot the downfall of those who served the Source
    of Hope.

You sent Moses, your servant;
Aaron, whom you had chosen from the rest.

You placed within them words and signs,
performed wonders in the land of Cham.

You sent forth darkness and covered the land with
    night.
The people did not sway from your word.

You transformed the waters of Egypt to blood
and killed their fish.

You made frogs swarm their land,
entering the chambers of their kings.

You spoke and stinging flies came,
lice spread throughout their gates.

You turned their rain to hail,
breathed forth fire to blaze across their land.

You struck both their vine and fig tree,
shattered saplings within their fences.

You spoke and swarms of locusts came,
devastating locusts beyond number.

They consumed every blade of grass,
devouring the fruit of their soil.

You struck down all their firstborn,
that which was the source of their strength.

You brought the Israelites out with silver and gold;
among your tribes there was not one who stumbled.

Egypt rejoiced when they were gone,
for a great dread was removed from each face.

You spread out a cloud to cover your people,
a fire to illumine the night.

They asked and you brought quail.
With bread from the sky, you satisfied their
    cravings.

You opened a rock, and water gushed forth.
It flowed through dry riverbeds freely.

For you remembered your holy word
and Abraham, your servant.

You led forth your people with joy,
your chosen ones with a cry of delight.

You gave them new lands,
earth on which to labor
among other nations—

for they kept to your rituals
and preserved the wisdom of your teaching.

Praise God.

Psalm 106

Praise God.

Give thanks to the Creator for all that is good.
Your kindness exists forever.

Who can put into words
your eternal commitment?
Who can make heard the entirety of your praise?

Blessed is the one who upholds justice,
who acts rightly at all times.

Remember me, God,
in your providence over the nation.

Watch over me with your protection,
so I can see the happiness
of those who love you—

rejoicing in the joy of your people,
praise along with those who have chosen you as their
    own.

We went astray like those who came before us;
we twisted away from God; we caused harm.

Our ancestors who dwelled in Egypt—
they didn't understand your wonders.

They failed to recall your many acts of love.
They rebelled at the ocean's edge,
balked at the Sea of Reeds.

But you saved them for the sake of your message,
in order to make known your strength.

You rebuked the Sea of Reeds, and it became dry
    land.
You led them through the depths
as you did later in the desert.

You saved them from the hand
of those who denied their humanity,

rescued them from the grasp
of those who wished them harm.

The water covered those who oppressed them;
not one remained alive.

Then they trusted your words
and sang out your praise.

But swiftly they forgot your acts;
they didn't bother to wait for your counsel.

They became wracked with desires in the desert,
tested you in desolate sand.

You gave them all they asked for,
but their souls remained hungry.

They were jealous of Moses in the camp,
of Aaron, your holy servant.

The earth opened and swallowed Datan.
It covered the congregation of Aviram.

A fire blazed through their followers.
Its torch flame ignited those who did wrong.

They fashioned a calf at Horev,
bowed down before molten metal.

They exchanged self-respect
for the image of an ox eating grass.

They forgot God, the one who saved them,
who accomplished great wonders in Egypt,

miracles in the land of Cham,
staggering spectacles at the Sea of Reeds.

You said you would have destroyed them
had not Moses, your chosen one, stood in the valley
to calm your anger from flattening them to the ground.

They refused the land of delight.
They had no trust in your word.

They murmured in their tents,
did not listen to the voice of their Upholder.

You lifted up your hand against them
to let them perish in the desert,

to make their children fall to other nations,
scattering them across foreign lands.

They clung like lovers to Baal Peor,
ate sacrifices to the dead.

They angered you with their actions,
and a plague split through their midst.

Pinchas stood and prayed
until the plague was brought to a halt.

It was thought to be an act of virtue
by generation after generation, forever.

They stirred up your wrath at the Waters of
    Contention,
brought punishment upon Moses on their
    account.

They made his soul go astray,
so he spoke rashly with his lips.

They didn't clear a path through the nations
as you had told them to do.

They mingled with the people
and studied their ways.

They served false gods that bring sorrow,
which became for them a snare.

They sacrificed their sons and daughters
to demons that demanded destruction.

They poured out innocent blood, blood of their
    own children
sacrificed to idols of Canaan,
and the land was polluted with blood.

They defiled themselves with their deeds,
became adulterers with repeated offense.

And your anger burned against the people.
You turned away from those who defied your will.

You gave them over to other nations
to be ruled in cruelty by those who despised them.

The oppressors weighed heavily against them,
making them buckle under their hand.

Time after time you rescued them,
but they rebelled with wrong counsel,
fell down through mistaken turns.

But upon hearing their cries, you saw their affliction.
You remembered your covenant for their sake,
comforted them because of the extent of your love.

You turned the hearts of their captors to compassion.

Save us, God; gather us from the nations—
to give thanks to your Holy Name,
to glorify you with praises.

We are awed before you, Eternal One, God of Israel,
from eternity until eternity,

and let all the people say amen.

Praise God.

Psalm 107

Give thanks to the Creator for all that is good;
your kindness exists forever.

Those who were rescued will proclaim it,
those who you redeemed from the hand of distress.

From distant lands you gathered them in,
from the place of sunrise
to the place where the sun is swallowed by dark,
from the north to the sea's border of sand.

They strayed from you in the desert,
frightened by the desolate landscape of their path.

A city to dwell in they could not find.
Their hunger grew unquenchable, they thirsted until
    dry,
their souls grew faint within.

They cried out to you about all that made quiver their
    minds.
From all their constraints, you lifted them safely away.

You helped them traverse a straight path,
to walk toward a city where they could peacefully
    dwell.

Pour out thanks for God's kindness,
your wonders to humankind.

You satisfied souls wracked with thirst;
hungry souls were filled with plenty—

those who dwelled in darkness and death's shadow,
shackled by anguish and iron,

for they had rebelled against your word,
scorned the counsel of the Most High.

You humbled their hearts with hard labor.
They stumbled and could find none to help.

Then they cried out to you about all that made quiver
    their minds.
From all their constraints, you lifted them safely away.

You brought them out from darkness and death's
    shadow,
broke off the shackles that kept them constrained.

Pour out thanks for God's kindness,
your wonders to humankind.

For you smashed down copper doors,
hacked off their iron bolts.

The foolish—because of their defiant, twisted road
they strayed from God.

All they ate made them queasy.
They grew faint, approaching the gateway of death.

And they called out to you about all that made quiver
     their minds.
From all their constraints, you lifted them safely away.

You sent forth your word and healed them,
you helped them escape destruction.

Pour out thanks for God's kindness,
your wonders to humankind.

Let the ones who go down to the sea in boats,
those who work on tumultuous waters,

offer sacrifices of thanksgiving,
proclaim your deeds with joyous song.

They saw your acts,
your wonders in the depths of the sea.

When you speak, the raging wind stands attentive,
the waves lift toward you their froth.

They rise toward heaven, they plunge to the depths.
Their souls melt with the terrible sight.

They lurch and stagger as though drunk.
All their wisdom is swallowed by fear.

And they cried out to you about all that made quiver
    their minds.
From all their constraints, you lifted them safely away.

You made the storm recoil into silence,
the waves became hushed.

They rejoiced, for it grew quiet;
you guided them toward a city
where they could peaceably dwell.

Pour out thanks for God's kindness,
your wonders to humankind.

They exalted you wherever people gather;
the elderly praised you inside their homes.

You transformed rivers to desert,
springs of water to thirsty earth,

a land of fruit to plains of salt,
because of the wrongs of those who lived there.

You turned deserts to swampland,
barren earth to wells that bring forth water.

In that place you settled the famished;
they established a city in which to live.

They sprinkled seed in the fields
and planted vineyards that yielded plentiful fruit.

The women, too, yielded good harvest;
their livestock did not decrease.

Later they began dying off and knuckling over;
their wealth brought them sorrow and groans.

You reject those greedy for money,
making them stumble in confusion, without a path.

You lift the poor from their suffering,
guide whole families like a flock of sheep.

Those who recognize your path will see and rejoice;
the unjust will all shut their mouths in silence.

Who is wise? Those who preserve these truths,
who understand in their depths the steadfast kindness
    of God.

Psalm 108

A SONG, A PSALM OF DAVID.

My heart is sturdy, God.

I will sing and make melodies
from the place where my glory resides.

Awake, O lyre and harp,
with you I will awaken the dawn.

I will proclaim thanks to you among the nations,
    my Upholder,
I will sing of you in every place people dwell.

Because towering above the heavens is your kindness;
your constancy reaches the highest level of clouds.

Lift yourself above the heavens, God—
spread over all the earth is your glory.

That your beloved ones be spared destruction,
reach out your right hand in response.

You spoke in holiness; I will exult in your word:

*I will divide Shechem and measure the valley of
    Sukkot.*

Gilead belongs to me, and mine is Menashe.
Ephraim is a stronghold for my head,
Judah is engraved upon me forever.

Moab is the basin in which I wash myself.
Upon Edom I will thrust my shoe.

Philistia will be broken asunder.

Who will bear me along to an enclosed city?
Who will lead me to Edom?

Is it not you, God, who has forsaken us?
Do you go with us when we march off to war?

Give us help from our affliction;
humankind is useless when it comes to salvation.

Only with you do we achieve strength;
only you can trample our oppressors to the ground.

Psalm 109

FOR THE CONDUCTOR OF THE ETERNAL SYMPHONY,
BY DAVID, A PSALM.

God whom I praise, don't remain silent.

For the mouths of wrongful deceivers
have opened against me.

They speak in a language of lies.

Words of their hatred surround me;
they clash against me without cause.
In return for my love, they offer obstruction.

But I myself am prayer.

They heap upon me harm in exchange for kindness,
hatred in exchange for love.

Place a warrior above them,
let the great accuser stand to their right.

When they are judged, let them leave condemned;
let their prayer be futile.

Let their days be few; let another replace their
    position.
Let their children become orphans, their wives
    widows.

Let their children wander and beg,
seeking food in desolate places.

May a creditor strike all that they own,
a stranger plunder their wealth.

May there be none who reach out to their family,
none who offer their children help.

May all who come after them be cut off from their
    people;
in the next generation, may God erase their names.

The sin of their fathers will be remembered by the
    Holy One,
and the wrongs of their mothers will not be wiped
    away.

They will be before God always,
but their memory will vanish from the earth.

Because they didn't remember to do kindness,
pursuing instead the poor and dejected,
the timid of heart, to kill them.

And just as they loved to curse others, now it has
    come to them.
They took no pleasure in blessing, and so it remains
    from them distant.

They dressed in curse as though with a garment;
it flowed like water through their veins,
like oil through their bones.

May it be for them like suffocating clothes,
like a belt that strangles the waist.

May such be the plight of those who oppose you,
those who speak brutality to my soul.

But you, God, are my Upholder.
Do with me as befits your name.

Because your kindness is good,
lift me from harm.

I am afflicted and poor;
my heart is hollow inside.

Like a stretched shadow, I am nearly gone;
I have been flung away like a locust.

My knees are weak from fasting,
my flesh lean from lack of food.

I have been an object of scorn;
those who look at me shake their heads.

Help me, Eternal, my God.
Save me in keeping with your kindness.

They will know that it is your hand that saves,
that you, God, have done it.

They may curse, but you will bless.

They rise up and fall disgraced,
but your servant will have lasting joy.

My obstructers will be clothed in humiliation,
wrapped in humiliation like a shawl.

I will thank you with my mouth,
praising your holy presence
wherever people gather.

For you stand at the right hand of the helpless
to save their soul
from those who would condemn it to death.

Psalm 110

By David, a psalm, a pronouncement of God,
the Upholder.

Wait at my right
until I make your enemies your footstool.

The staff of your strength
I will send you from Zion.

Be powerful amidst what frightens you.
Your nation will offer help on the day
you gather forces on the holy mountain.

From the womb's darkness,
from the first burst into dawn of life—
to you belongs the dew of youth.

I have promised and will not prove false:
you will be priest forever,
as I vowed of Malchitzedek,
the virtuous king:

I am at your right side,
flinging aside kings on the day of my wrath.

I will judge nations piled high with corpses,
crushing leaders of those lands.

But you—from a river along the way, you will drink.
You will always lift your head high.

Psalm 111

Praise God!

I will thank the Holy One with all my heart—
in talking with the earnest,
and whenever people gather.

Your acts are vast beyond measure;
all who delight in them marvel at their power.

Majesty and splendor pour forth from creation;
your generosity endures for all time.

You crafted your wonders to last forever;
you overflow with compassion and grace.

You give sustenance to those who revere you,
those who keep your covenant always in mind.

The power of your deeds, you conveyed to your
    people,
giving them land on which to dwell.

The works of your hand are truth and justice;
your protection is worthy of trust—

always dependable, fashioned from clarity and truth.

You sent word to your nation,
promising your covenant would continue forever.

Holy and awesome is the Infinite Name.

The beginning of wisdom is wonder at God,
good knowledge for all who serve you.
Your praise stands present forever.

Psalm 112

Praise God!

Content are the ones who hold the Creator in wonder.
In your direction is found continual delight.

Their offspring will be mighty in the land;
a generation of purpose, they will be blessed.

Abundance and treasure fill their homes.
Their righteousness is always present.

For the goodhearted, light shines even in dark;
you are full of grace, compassion, and justice.

Praiseworthy are those who give freely and lend,
who fulfill all their words with action.

For eternity they will never stumble.
Memory of their righteousness will last for all time.

When word comes of danger, they will not fear.
Their hearts will be firm, steadfast in God's presence.

With heart upheld by the Creator,
they will not be frightened;

in time, they will see their oppressors
brought to justice.

Those who share their wealth with the poor,
their love of humanity stands illumined forever.

Their faces will glow, lifted high with glory.

Those who simmer with hatred will see and grow
angry;
gnashing their teeth, they will melt away.

All desires of the wrongful
will ultimately be lost.

Psalm 113

Halleluyah!

Shine forth praises to God.

Give praise, you who serve the Creator!
Give praise to the Holy Name.

May the name of the Eternal be knelt to in wonder,
from now until the end of time.

From the east where the sun rises
to the place where it is swallowed by dark,
may the Holy Name be blessed.

You are high above all nations;
spread over the whole sky is your glory.

Who is like you, our Creator,
the one who sits among angels on a heavenly throne,

who comes down low to bear witness
to the sky and to the earth?

You raise the downtrodden from dust,
lift the desperate from trash heaps

to seat them at a table of the more wealthy,
the more wealthy from among their people—

making the woman who has not given birth
feel like a joyful mother of children.

Shine forth praises to God!

Halleluyah.

Psalm 114

When Israel went forth from Egypt,
the house of Jacob from those of foreign tongue,

Judah became your holy one,
Israel the place of your governance.

The ocean saw and fled;
the Jordan flowed backward.

The mountains skipped like rams,
the foothills like flocks of sheep.

What is wrong with you, sea, that you flee?
And Jordan, that you flow backward?

Mountains, why do you skip like rams?
Foothills, why take fright like sheep?

Before the Holy Presence, the earth trembles,
before the God of Jacob—

the one who changes rock into flowing pools,
flint into wellsprings of water.

Psalm 115

Not to us, God, not to us,
but to your name belongs glory—

because of your kindness
and your constancy in our lives.

Why do nations ask, "Where is their Savior?"
Our God is in heaven; all the Eternal desires has been
    done.

Their idols of silver and gold lead to sadness,
craft of a human hand.

They have mouths, but cannot speak,
eyes, but cannot see,

ears, but do not hear,
a nose, but smell no fragrance.

They have hands, but do not feel,
legs, but cannot walk.
No utterance of wisdom comes from their throat.

Like them will their makers become,
all who trust in false objects of praise.

Israel—trust in God.
The Creator is your help and your shield.

House of Aaron, trust in God.
The Creator is your help and your shield.

You who behold the Holy with wonder, trust in God.
The Creator is your help and your shield.

Remember us, God, and bless us—

blessing the house of Israel,
blessing the house of Aaron,

blessing all who truly see God—
the unknown along with the named.

The Holy One will add to your joy,
blessing you and all of your children.

You are already blessed by the Creator,
maker of heaven and earth.

The heavens are the heavens of God;
the earth belongs to us creatures.

The dead cannot praise the Source of Life,
those who go down to the depths into silence.

But we stand in wonder of your blessings,
from now until the end of time.

Praise God!

Psalm 116

I love you, God, for you listen to my voice,
my prayers for solace in times of need.

Because you leaned your ear toward me with
    kindness,
I will call out to you all of my days.

The rope of death circled around me;
constrictions of the underworld tracked me down.

Narrowness of circumstance and grief—
wherever I looked I would find them.

But I would call out your name—
"Please, God, save me!"

Generous and just, our Hope is full of compassion.

You keep watch over the willing.
I sank to low depths, but you saved me.

Return, my soul, to a place of rest,
for the Eternal will sustain you with kindness.

God rescued me from death,
my eyes from drowning in sadness,
my foot from stumbling.

I will walk before the Holy One in the land of the
    living.

I kept a corner of faith even when I said:
"My suffering is beyond measure."

Too quickly I proclaimed while afraid:
"All humanity is full of betrayal."

With what can I repay you, God,
for all your kindness to me?

A cup of gratitude I lift up,
crying your name out in praise,

upholding my vows to you
in sight of all your people.

Sorrowful in your eyes
is the death of your faithful.

I plead with you, God, for I am your servant;
your servant, offspring of those loyal to your name.

You opened my tight and hard-knot places.
To you I will bring offerings of thanks;

I will cry out your name in praise,
upholding my vows to you
in sight of all your people—

in the courtyards of the house of worship,
in the midst of Jerusalem—praise God!

Psalm 117

Shine praises upon God, all nations;
let all the world approach you with worship.

For your love has won us over;
your loyalty exists for all time—praise God.

Psalm 118

Give thanks to God for compassion;
your kindness exists forever.

Let Israel proclaim it:
your kindness exists forever.

Let the house of Aaron proclaim it:
your kindness exists forever.

Let those who hold you in awe proclaim it:
your kindness exists forever.

From a place of constriction, I called to you,
and you answered with an expanse of heavenly
    presence.

God is with me, I have no fear;
what can a mere mortal do to me?

Your presence is known through all who help me;
with them, I can look danger squarely in the face.

It is better to take refuge in you
than trust in a mortal.

It is better to take refuge in you
than trust in wealth.

All the nations surrounded me—
in the name of my Protector, I circumcised their heart.

They moved closer and pushed toward me from
    afar—
in the name of my Protector, I circumcised their heart.

They swarmed like bees;
they burned me like fire with thorns—
in the name of my Protector, I circumcised their heart.

They pushed me hard, hoping I would fall,
but the Holy One helped me stand straight.

My strength and my song is God,
source of my salvation.

Cry with joy at redemption in the tents of the
    righteous;
your hand is steadfast with strength.

The right arm of the Holy is raised;
your hand is steadfast with strength.

I will not die; I will live—
to tell the deeds of the Living God.

You reproved me, but did not hand me over to death.

Open for me the gates of justice;
I will enter to give thanks to your name.

This is the gateway to the Holy;
only the righteous can enter.

I will give thanks to you, for you humbled me;
only then could you become my source of help.

The rock rejected by builders
has become the cornerstone of faith.

Coming from the Creator,
it was, in our eyes, a wonder.

This is the day that our Source of Joy has made;
Let us exult and rejoice in it.

Save us, God!
Help us succeed, our Upholder!

Welcome to all who come in your name;
we bless you from the sanctuary of God.

You, God, are mighty, illumining the world.

Bind the holiday offering with ropes;
bring it to the radiance of the altar.

You are my Source of Strength and I will thank you.
You are my God, and I will raise your name in praise.

Give thanks to God for compassion;
your kindness exists forever.

Psalm 119

Joyful are those whose path is complete,
who walk in your teaching.

Joyful are those who uphold your testimony;
with full heart they seek you out.

They do not labor for flawed goals;
they walk the path toward fulfillment.

You have commanded us often
to hold fast to your service.

If only I could straighten my footsteps
to hold fast to your statutes,
I would never be ashamed to gaze upon your will.

I will thank you with a clear heart
as I learn the ways of your righteousness.

Your eternal laws—I will keep them.
Don't abandon me completely.

How can a child make clear her path?
By paying attention to her wanderings
in keeping with your word.

With all my heart muscle, I have sought you.
Let me not wander from the orchard of your will.

In my mind I have fortified your phrases,
so I would not fall away from your purpose.

Praised are you, Unnamable One,
for revealing the mystery of your law.

With my lips I will recount
all the judgments of your mouth.

When I witnessed your testimony, I rejoiced,
as though I had received all the world's riches.

I will converse of your charge
and gaze on your paths.

I will delight in your eternal statutes,
never forgetting your word.

Show your servant fruit of your kindness;
I live in order to keep your teaching.

Throw the veil from my eyes that I might see
the wonders of your knowledge.

I am a stranger in the land;
don't hide from me the nuances of your will.

My soul is crushed into shards
from longing every moment for your justice.

You rebuke those who willfully defy you,
along with those who stray without intention from
    your will.

Remove scorn and contempt from me
for I have upheld evidence of your presence.

Even as royalty sat testifying against me,
your servant spoke loyally of your truths.

Your testimonies are my obsession;
like people, they give me good counsel.

My soul has clung to dust;
grant me a new spirit in keeping with your word.

I have confided to you the confusions of my path,
and you responded;
teach me the mysteries of your law.

The path of your service—help me understand it.
Then I will speak of your wonders.

My soul wept, melting with grief;
keep me upright in accordance with your word.

A false path, turn it far from me;
place before me instead the gift of your wisdom.

I have freely chosen a way of faith.
I have tried to become equal
to the way of your justice.

I have clung to your testimonies—
God, don't let me fall to self-loathing.

The way of your will, I run toward it,
for you have broadened my heart.

Throw toward me, God, the path of your statutes,
and I will treasure it by holding fast with my
    footsteps.

Let me know its nuances, and I will uphold your
    teaching.
I will keep it with the fullness of my heart.

Show me how to walk on the paths of your will
because in them I have found my delight.

Bend my heart to your testimony
and not toward selfish greed.

Turn my eyes from looking too closely
at that which leads to futility.
In your path, help me live.

Uphold your promise to your servant,
the one who holds you in awe.

Turn away scorn from me, that which I dread,
for your decisions help cultivate goodness.

Behold—I have yearned to do your service.
In your justice, help me live.

May your love come toward me,
your salvation be in keeping with your speech.

I will respond to those who scorn me,
for in your word I have trusted.

Don't take away truth from my mouth,
for I have longed to perform your justice.

I will always hold fast to your teaching,
forever, under testimony of time.

I will walk on wide paths,
for I have sought to perform your service.

Before kings, I will speak testimony of you
and not be ashamed.

I will delight in your commandments,
the ones I have loved.

I will lift up my hands to do your will,
the commandments that bring me joy.

I will speak of your statutes.

Remember the word you gave your servant,
the one that has given me hope.

It has been my comfort in times of affliction,
for your promise has kept me alive.

Arrogant ones have scorned me completely,
but from your teaching I never pulled away.

I remember your loyalty to justice, God,
from the beginning of creation,
and take comfort.

This has been my life's story,
for I have immersed myself
in fulfilling your service.

I trembled with feverish sweat
on account of the wrongful who abandoned your
    teaching.

Your statutes were melodies for me
in the house of my fears.

I remembered your name in the night, God,
and kept fast to your teaching.

This I did because
I was resolute in your service.

You are my portion—
I have vowed to hold fast to your words.

I have longed for the softness of your face
with the entire strength of my heart.

Give to me with compassion
in accordance with your word.

I have reflected upon my paths
and will turn my legs to your testimony.

I hurried and did not linger
in fulfilling your will.

Ropes of the wrongful encompassed me,
but I never forgot your teaching.

In the middle of the night, I arise,
thanking you for the justice of your judgments.

I am friend to all who hold you in awe,
to those who hold fast to your service.

Your acts of kindness, Holy One, fill the earth.
Your eternal law instructs me.

You have provided good for your servant
in keeping with your speech.

Reason is worthy, so teach me knowledge,
for I have believed in your will.

Before I suffered, I erred without knowing.
And now—I hold fast to your word.

You are good and bring about goodness—
teach me the essence of your mysterious ways.

The arrogant sinners smeared me with lies,
but with all my heart I upheld your service.

Their heart is swollen like fat,
but I have obsessed over your teachings.

My suffering has brought me good;
only through hardship
have I learned the bedrock of your truth.

The teaching of your mouth is pleasurable to me,
better than a thousand pieces of gold and silver.

Your hands formed me and gave me direction.
Help me understand so I can learn your will.

Those who are awed by you saw me and rejoiced—
because I wait for your word.

I know, God, that your judgments are rightful;
you afflicted me so that I could learn faith.

May your kindness comfort me,
as you promised your servant.

When your compassion rises toward me,
I am brought back to life,
for I am enthralled with your teaching.

The ones who willfully injure others will be
    ashamed,
for they distort me with lies.

I will continue to speak of your service.

Whoever is awed by you will return to my side;
they will learn testimony of your presence.

May my heart be pure in fulfilling your precepts;
then I will never become ashamed.

My soul grows dim waiting for your word.
My eyes are extinguished by your promise,
saying, "When will you come to comfort me?"

I have been like a wineskin shriveled in smoke,
but I never forgot your statutes.

How many days will your servant endure?
How long until you bring my pursuers to justice?

The wrongful dug pits for me
in contradiction with your word.

Your commandments to consider others
are the basis of faith.
They pursue me with lies—help!

They nearly destroyed me from the earth,
but I never abandoned your service.

In keeping with your love, restore me to life,
and I will hold fast to the testimony of your mouth.

You last forever—your word stands firm in the sky.

From generation to generation you remain faithful.
You established the earth and it continues to exist.

To fulfill your justice heaven and earth stand today,
for all of creation are your servants.

Had I not immersed myself in your teaching,
I would have died in my affliction.

For all of time I will never forget to serve you,
for that is what kept me alive.

I am yours—save me!
For I have sought to do your will.

The wrongful planned to destroy me,
but I contemplate evidence of your existence.

To every perfection, I have seen a limit,
but your will is wide beyond measure.

How I have loved your wisdom!
I converse about it all day long.

Through your commandments
I become wiser than my enemies
because your words are with me all the time.

From all my teachers I learned something of use.
Testimonies of your existence have been the essence
    of my talk.

May I learn understanding from my elders,
for I have endeavored to follow your will.

From every path of wrong, I have restrained my feet
in order to hold fast to your word.

I have not swayed from your ways of justice,
for you showed me how to live in your light.

How sweet are your words to my palate,
better than honey to my tongue.

In carrying out your service I gain understanding;
I despise every path of lies.

Your words are a candle for my feet, a light for my
     footpath.

I made an oath and will fulfill it—
to uphold your righteous judgments.

I have been afflicted beyond measure—
God, return me to life with your word.

The offerings of my mouth are freely given;
please accept them, Creator,
and teach me the ways of your justice.

My life is always fragile in my hand,
but your teachings I never forget.

The wrongful laid a trap for me,
but I never strayed from your service.

I inherited proofs of you that will hold forever,
for they are what makes my heart spring with joy.

I stretched out my will to keep your absolute statutes,
keep them always, because by you they were given.

I despise the halfhearted,
but your wisdom I love.

You are my concealment and my shield.
I have waited for your word.

Turn away from me, you who cause harm,
so I can uphold the will of my Upholder.

Support me as you promised, and I will live;
don't let me fall ashamed in my hope.

Nourish me, and I will be saved;
I will gaze upon your statutes always.

You toss to the side all who stray from your precepts,
for they plot a perversion of truth.

You removed all the wrongful from the earth—
I have loved testimonies of your truth.

My flesh shuddered from fear of you
and I was afraid of your judgments.

I have performed acts of justice and righteousness;
don't place me among those who degrade.

Your servant offers a pledge to do good.
Don't let the arrogant abuse me.

My eyes grow dim, waiting for your salvation,
longing for the promise of your justice.

Do with your servant in keeping with your kindness;
teach me your inscrutable laws.

I am your servant—enlighten me
so I can learn testimonies of your truth.

There is a time for God to act;
they shattered your teachings.

And so I have loved your commandments
more than gold, more than the finest gold in
    abundance.

And so, your charges—I pronounced them all just.
Every road of deception I despised.

Wonders are testimonies of your existence,
and so my soul clings to them tightly.

The doorways of your words illumine,
making the simple understand.

I opened my mouth, my breathing labored,
for I yearned to perform your will.

Turn toward me and pour forth your kindness,
as is rightful toward those who love your name.

Ready my footsteps toward your word;
don't let wrongfulness overtake my wandering.

Redeem me from human oppression
and I will gladly perform your service.

Let your face shine from within your servant
teach me your statutes.

Water streamed from my eyes,
because they did not follow your teaching.

You commanded your testimonies to be just
and they gave me great faith.

My jealousy annihilates me,
for my oppressors have forgotten your words.

Your promise is refined as purest metal
and your servant loves it completely.

I am young and despised,
but I have not forgotten your service.

Your justice is rightful forever,
and your wisdom is profoundest truth.

Anguish and anxiety found me,
but I found delight in your will.

Testimonies of your existence are relevant forever—
help me understand them and I will live.

I cried out with all my heart—
you answered me.

I will keep fast to your statutes.

I called upon you—save me!
I held close to the proof of your existence.

I arose before twilight and cried out for help.
I longed for your word of response.

My eyes awoke before the night watches
to meditate upon your word.

Listen to my voice in keeping with your kindness.
God, as befits your justice, help me live!

Those who pursue harm narrow closer.
From your teaching they remain far away.

You are close, God, and all your commandments
come from the flood of your truth.

I knew of you even before I had evidence of your acts,
for you made them a foundation forever.

See my affliction and lift me from it.
For your teaching I have not forgotten.

Contend my cause and make me again whole;
with your word, return me to life.

Salvation remains far from the wrongful,
for they do not seek your eternal law.

Many are my pursuers and sources of anguish;
from your testimonies I have not fled away.

I saw those who betrayed me, and felt loathing
because they refused to follow your word.

Look! Because I have loved your service, God,
in your kindness help me to live.

The first of your words is truth.
All your judgments point to what is right.

Princes pursued me for no reason;
because of your words, my heart did not fear.

I am joyful because of your word,
like one who stumbles on great treasure.

I have despised lies and found them abhorrent,
but your teachings I have always loved.

Seven times a day I praise you,
for your judgments are eternally just.

Great peace descends on those who love your wisdom.
They have no obstacle over which to fall.

I looked for your saving power with hope, God,
and performed with pleasure your will.

My soul held fast to testimonies of your existence.
I have loved each of them deeply.

Let my cry of joy approach your presence, God;
in keeping with your word, help me understand.

May my plea for compassion come before your face.
In keeping with your promise, lift me away.

My lips will overflow with praise,
for you have taught me the mysteries of your law.

My tongue will respond with your words,
for all of your will is toward justice.

May your hand be there to assist me,
for I have chosen the principles of your service.

I yearn for your salvation, God,
and immerse myself in your teaching.

Let my soul live, and it will praise you—
may your judgments always be my help.

I have wandered away like a lost sheep—
seek out your servant!

For I have not forgotten your will.

Psalm 120

A SONG OF UPLIFT.

In my constriction I called out to the Source of
    Compassion,
and you answered.

God, lift away my soul's blood
from lips that speak lies,
from a tongue that craves corruption.

What will it give you? How will you profit
from a mouth that speaks falsely?

The arrows of the mighty
are sharpened with coals of hardened brushwood.

Oh, so many years of drawn-out wandering!
I dwelt so long in darkened tents
craving a home.

For so long my soul has dwelt
with despisers of peace.

I myself am peace, but when I speak
they ready themselves for war.

Psalm 121

A SONG OF UPLIFT.

I lift my eyes to the mountains.
From where will my help come?

My only help comes from God,
the one who shaped heaven and earth,
who made each crevice, who smoothed each stone.

God will not allow your foot to stumble;
the One who watches over you will not drowse off
    to sleep.

Behold! The Holy One does not slumber and does not
    sleep,
the one who nurtures Israel through its darkest nights.

God is the one who watches over you,
the shade under your right hand,
whenever you move it up or place it down.

By day the sun will not strike you,
nor the moon weaken you at night.

The Upholder will protect you from every harm;
the Eternal Shield will keep constant watch over your
    soul.

God will guard your going out and coming in,
from now until the end of time. Amen.

Psalm 122

A SONG OF UPLIFT,
BY DAVID.

My joy overflowed when they said to me,
"Let us go to the house of God."

Our feet stood at your gates, Jerusalem.
Jerusalem—the city composed by human hands,
a city in which all are one.

For there the tribes ascended, the tribes of the
        Holy One—
a testimony by Israel, giving thanks to God's name.

For that was where they sat on thrones in judgment,
thrones of the house of David.

Pray for peace in Jerusalem,
contentment for all who love you.

May there be peace in your ramparts,
tranquility in your sanctuaries.

For the sake of my brothers and sisters
I will speak words of peace to you,

for the sake of your holy dwelling, God,
I will pursue good for the sake of all.

Psalm 123

A SONG OF UPLIFT.

To you I lift up my gaze,
to the one who dwells in heaven.

Look! Like the eyes of devoted workers
looking toward their master's hand,

like the eyes of a maidservant
fixed on her mistress's hand—

so have our eyes have turned toward you, our God,
waiting until you turn toward us with compassion.

Consider us with kindness, Holy One!
For we overflow with the world's contempt.

Our soul floods with derision
from those who live in ease;

disdain of those who think themselves unreachable,
towering above the rest.

Psalm 124

A SONG OF UPLIFT, BY DAVID.

If not for God who acted on our behalf—
let Israel proclaim it—

if not for God who was with us
when people rose up against us in war,

they would have swallowed us alive
in the blaze of their rage.

The water would have flooded us,
a river would have flowed over our soul.

Turbulent waves would have suffocated us,
drowning out our life.

Praised is God,
who refused to give us
as carnage to their teeth.

We escaped with our lives
like a bird from a baited snare.

The trap broke and we flew toward freedom.

Our only help comes in the name of God,
maker of heaven and earth.

Psalm 125

A SONG OF UPLIFT.

Those who trust you, God, are like Mount Zion—
which does not crumble, but continues forever.

Jerusalem—mountains wrap around it,
just as you enfold your people
from now until the end of time.

For the Creator does not let a group of the wrongful
rest in land of the righteous,

so hands of the righteous
are not tempted toward harm.

Provide goodness, God, for those who are good,
and give to the steadfast their heart's content—

but for those who grow increasingly twisted,
let them walk in their tumultuous deeds.

Peace be to those who struggle with God.

Psalm 126

A SONG OF UPLIFT.

When the Redeemer returns the exiles to Zion
we will have been like dreamers.

Then our mouths will overflow with laughter,
our tongues with cries of joy.

Then it will be said among the nations:
"God has acted with grandeur
on behalf of these people."

God will act with wonder toward *us*;
the thought fills us with joy.

The Holy One has glorified us by name—
we will be as though having been
in the divine presence throughout.

Return us, God, from our exile
like sudden streambeds in the Negev.

Those who plant seeds with tears of sorrow
will gather the harvest with songs of joy.

The one who walks even while weeping,
lifting the seed as he goes,

will return with gladness,
carrying his sheaves of corn.

Psalm 127

A Song of Uplift,
by Solomon.

If God does not build a house,
its builders labor upon it in vain.

If God does not keep guard over a city,
it is futile for the watchman to keep awake.

It is useless—you who rise at dawn,
who stay up late,
who eat the bread of sadness.

But, yes, in the end God will give sleep to the
     faithful.
Behold—children are a holy gift.

The reward of the just is the fruit of their womb.
Like arrows in the hand of a warrior,
so are children given birth to when young.

Happy is the warrior who fills his quiver with them—
he will not be ashamed.

Because his children will make peace,
speaking softly to the enemies at the gate.

Psalm 128

A SONG OF UPLIFT.

Joyous are those who are awed by God,
who walk contentedly on the path.

You will earn the toil of your hands,
You will eat in happiness and all will go well.

Your love will be like a fruitful vine
in the hidden rooms of your house.

Your children will be like olives,
planted shoots sprouting around your table.

See!—for that is the way a person is blessed,
one awed by the wonder of God.

The Upholder will bless you from Zion
and you will gaze on the hope of Jerusalem
all the days of your life.

You will see your children give birth to children,
and peace in the land of Israel.

Psalm 129

A SONG OF UPLIFT.

Many are the times they pressed against me—
from the time of my youth—

let Israel proclaim it.

Many are the times they pressed against me
from the time of my youth—

but they could not defeat me completely.

Upon my back the engravers ploughed and carved.
They lengthened the hours for labor.

You understand what is right, God—
you cut the rope of the wrongful in half.

May they be ashamed and fall backward,
those who despise Zion.

May they be like grass on the rooftops
that grows withered before it is plucked,

so the harvester cannot fill his palm with it,
nor carry sheaves of wheat against his chest.

And for those who fail to recognize
the blessing of God upon all of us,
we bless you in the name of God.

Psalm 130

A SONG OF UPLIFT.

From the fathomless deep I have called to you, God.
Listen to the innermost depths of my voice.

Open your ears to the sound of my cry.
If you kept a record of guilt, my Source of Strength,
who could remain standing?

For with you is forgiveness;
from it, we learn how to hold you in wonder.

I look for you, my soul looks for you wildly,
I wait for your word of response.

My soul longs for you
more than the watchman at the gate longs for
    morning,

more than the tired watchman at the gate
longs for the first flicker of dawn.

Let Israel put its hope in God,
for with you is a storehouse of kindness,
and with the Holy One redemption abounds.

You will redeem Israel
from all its guilt and confusion and sin.

Psalm 131

A SONG OF UPLIFT, BY DAVID.

God, my heart is not swollen,
nor my eyes lifted high.

I haven't walked too proudly
and didn't push to stand out.

Have I not steadied and silenced my soul
like a baby nursing upon its mother,
as though a baby were nursing upon me?

Yearn constantly, Israel, for God,
from now until the end of time.

Psalm 132

A SONG OF UPLIFT,
A PSALM, BY DAVID,
FOR GOD TO REMEMBER HIS SUFFERING,
BY ONE WHO SWORE AN OATH TO GOD,
WHO MADE A VOW TO THE INVINCIBLE STRENGTH OF
    JACOB.

I will not go into the tent of my house,
will not sit on my bed and lie down,

will not allow my eyes to sleep,
my eyelids to slumber

until I find a place for you,
a tabernacle for the Invincible Strength of Jacob.

Behold—we heard of it in Euphrates,
we found it in a field surrounded by forest.

We will come to your tabernacle,
bow down before the footstool of your feet.

Rise up, God, to a place of resting,
you and the ark of your strength.

Your priests will clothe themselves in justice;
the devoted will sing out in joy.

For the sake of David, your servant,
don't turn away your future hope.

You swore to David an immutable truth—
don't turn back from your word:

On your throne, I will set the fruit of your loins.

If your children keep my covenant,
I will teach them testimony of my existence.

Your children's children will also endure forever,
ruling in holiness because of you.

For the Eternal chose Zion,
longing for it as a place upon which to dwell:

This is my resting place, existing forever.
Here I will settle, for it is the place for which I yearned.

I will bless her abundantly with all her needs,
satisfy her poor with bread.

Her priests I will clothe with salvation;
the devoted will sing out a great song.

There I will cause the ray of strength
to sprout from David.

I have arranged a candle for my anointed.
His enemies I will clothe in shame.

But upon him a crown will blossom,
shining perpetually bright.

Psalm 133

A SONG OF UPLIFT,
BY DAVID.

Behold! How sweet and pleasant
is a dwelling of brothers and sisters
who live together as one.

Like fine oil upon the head
running down the beard,
the beard of Aaron

that runs down the mouth of his garment,
like the dew of Hermon
running down the hillsides of Zion.

Because that is where God willed into existence
the blessing of eternal life.

Psalm 134

A Song of Uplift,
by David.

Behold—

be humbled,
all who serve the Eternal in wonder,

who stand in God's sanctuary
throughout the long nights.

Lift up your hands in holiness
and praise your Creator.

From Zion the Holy One will bless you,
maker of heaven and earth.

Psalm 135

Praise God!

Shine out praises to the heavenly name.
Let all who serve God praise their Creator,
all who stand in the house of the Eternal,
in the courtyards of the house of our Strength.

Give praise, for God is good.
Sing to the heavenly name, for it is pleasant.

For the Upholder chose Jacob as holy,
Israel as a treasured possession.

I know, God, that you are vast,
more powerful than all false objects of praise.

All that you desired, you have done,
in heaven and on earth,
in the sea and its deepest depths.

You lift up fog from the ends of the earth
and make thunderstorms to water the soil.

You bring forth wind from your storehouse of
      treasure.

You struck down the firstborn of Egypt,
from humankind to cattle and flocks.

You sent forth signs and wonders throughout the
    land—
to Pharaoh and all of his servants.

You struck down many nations,
and slew despotic kings:

Sichon, king of the Emorites,
and Og, king of Bashan,
along with all the kingdoms of Canaan.

You gave their land as inheritance,
inheritance to Israel, your nation.

Eternal One, we will call out your name forever.
Your memory lasts from one generation to the next.

For you judge your people justly,
your servants with tenderness and truth.

Other gods are silver and gold
and lead to sadness,
the work of a human hand.

They have a mouth, but cannot speak;
eyes, but cannot see.

They have ears, but cannot hear.
Neither is there breath in their mouths.

Like them will their makers become,
all who trust in them.

House of Israel, sing out your blessing to God.
House of Aaron, sing out your blessing to God.

House of Levi, sing out your blessing to God.
Those who are awed by God, sing out your blessing
   to God.

Blessed is the Creator from Zion,
the one who dwells in Jerusalem—praise God!

Psalm 136

>─◆─○─◆─◁

Give thanks to the Creator for all that is good—
   for God's kindness is toward the world.
Give thanks to the Judge of all judges—
   for God's kindness is toward the world.

Give thanks to the Foundation of foundations—
   for God's kindness is toward the world.
To the one who performs great miracles alone—
   for God's kindness is toward the world.

To the one who makes the sky with great wisdom—
   for God's kindness is toward the world.
To the one who spreads the earth over the sea—
   for God's kindness is toward the world.

To the one who makes great lights—
    for God's kindness is toward the world.
The sun to govern by day—
    for God's kindness is toward the world.

The moon and stars to govern by night—
    for God's kindness is toward the world.
The one who struck Egypt through their firstborn—
    for God's kindness is toward the world.

The one who brought out Israel from their midst—
    for God's kindness is toward the world.
With a strong hand and outstretched arm—
    for God's kindness is toward the world.

To the one who split the Sea of Reeds into parts—
    for God's kindness is toward the world.
Who helped Israel cross through its midst—
    for God's kindness is toward the world.

And threw Pharaoh and his army into its water—
    for God's kindness is toward the world.
To guide the people in the desert—
    for God's kindness is toward the world.

The one who struck down powerful kings—
    for God's kindness is toward the world.
And slew kings who seemed invincible—
    for God's kindness is toward the world.

Sichon, king of the Emorites—
    for God's kindness is toward the world.
Og, king of Bashan—
    for God's kindness is toward the world.

And gave their land as a portion—
    for God's kindness is toward the world.
A portion to Israel, your servant—
    for God's kindness is toward the world.

Who when we were low in spirit remembered us—
    for God's kindness is toward the world.
And broke us away from our oppressors—
    for God's kindness is toward the world.

Who gives food to all flesh—
    for God's kindness is toward the world.
Give thanks to the Power of the heavens—
    for God's kindness is toward the world.

Psalm 137

By the rivers of Babylon
there we sat down
and there we wept
when we remembered Zion.

On the willows along the shore we hung our harps,
  for there our captors demanded words of song.

Our mockers insisted upon gladness, saying,
"Sing for us a song of the Zion you love."

How can we sing a song of God
in a strange land?

If I ever forget you, Jerusalem
let my right hand grow numb,
let my tongue cling to the roof of my mouth,

if I do not remember,
if I fail to raise Jerusalem
above my highest joy.

Let the children of Edom remember God,
on the day of Jerusalem,

those who said:
"Lay it naked, strip it bare,
down to its very foundation."

O daughter of Babylon, ravaged one,
your wrongs have led you to suffer.

One day you, too, will see your brightest future
shattered against a rock.

Psalm 138

By David.

I will thank you with the fullness of my heart.
Before the Source of my Strength I will sing.

I will bow down before your holy chambers,
grateful for your presence, your love, and your truth.

Because your word has more worth
than any of the other names upon which we call.

On the day I cried out, you answered me,
emboldening me, giving my soul strength.

Rulers of the earth will all thank you, God,
when they hear the words of your mouth.

They will sing to you on your holy pathways,
for vast is our Creator's glory.

You are high, but see those who are low.
You know the mountains from afar.

If I walk into the thick of my sorrow,
you keep me alive—
against the wrath of my fears.

You send forth your hand;
your right arm saves me.

God—accomplish for me what I cannot finish.
God—your kindness endures forever.

Don't let the work of your hands grow weak.

Psalm 139

For the Conductor of the Eternal Symphony,
by David, a psalm.

God, you have searched out my deepest places;
you know what lies in my depth.

You know my sitting down and rising up.

You know how to shepherd me from afar.
My paths and night thoughts—you sift through them.

You know all my roads,
for there has been no word on my tongue
that—behold—you did not know it beforehand.

From front and behind you encompassed me;
you laid your hand upon me in protection.

Wondrous beyond words is your knowledge.
It remains inaccessible, beyond my grasp.

Where can I hide from your breath?
From before your presence, where can I flee?

If I ascend to heaven, there you are.

If I lie down in the grave—behold,
you are there, too.

If I lift myself on wings of sunrise,
if I dwell in the western sea,

there, also, your hand will guide me.
You hold me upright with the strength of your right
    arm.

I have said, "Surely darkness will bruise me,"
but suddenly night became a surrounding glow.

Even darkness does not darken you from me.
Night like day illumines,
Darkness and light—no difference.

For you know my deepest emotions.
You pulled me from my mother's womb—

I thank you, for your wonders are breathtaking,
your deeds a constant source of awe.

My soul knows it well.

My bones are not hidden from you,
the ones I was composed from in secret

when my body was woven together
in the deepest center of the earth.

Your eyes saw my embryo.
And in your Book of Wonders all is written.

Days were shaped and fashioned;
to you they are as one.

As for me—what will happen to those who love you,
    God?
How strong are the leaders who come bearing arms!

Were I to count them, they would outnumber the
    grains of sand.
I woke up—and again you were with me!

Won't you halt, God, inflictors of harm?
And those of bloodshed, turn them away?

The ones who invoke your name, scheming,
who lift in futility the words of your curse?

Is it not true, God, that I oppose those who oppose you?
And those who rise up against you, I reject?

Put to an end the hatred of the haters,
those who have made me their foe.

Search me out with shovel and torchlight, God;
know my heart by means of compassion.

Understand the turbulent branching of my thoughts.

See the road that brings me sadness,
and lead me instead on the path of eternal life.

Psalm 140

▷─┼◇┄○┄◇┼─◁

FOR THE CONDUCTOR OF THE ETERNAL SYMPHONY,
A PSALM OF DAVID.

Release me, God, from the heartless;
from those of violence, keep vigilant watch.

Those who scheme malice in their hearts—
every day they stir up wars.

They have sharpened their tongues like a snake;
a viper's poison trickles on their lips—Selah!

Protect me, God, from the unkind;
from those of violence, keep vigilant watch,
those who intend to make me stumble.

The haughty buried a snare for me, ropes to make
    me fall.
They spread out a net along the ditch;
they set traps for my feet—Selah!

I said to God: "You are the wellspring of my
    strength!"
Open your ears, Holy One, to my cry.

God, my Upholder, you are the strength behind
    my salvation.
You cover my head with comfort
on the day when bloodshed strikes.

Don't give in, my Creator, to wishes of the wrongful.
Don't let their scheming come to pass—
they will think themselves higher than you—Selah.

The heads of those who come intending harm—
let the dirt of their own lips cover them.

Let blazing coals hail down,
making them stumble into fire, into floods,
leaving them unable to rise.

A person with hateful tongue
will never be at peace in the land.

Those of violence—
their own evil will hunt them down
thrust upon thrust.

I know what God will do—
you stand up for the afflicted,
bringing down judgment on behalf of the poor.

Only the righteous are grateful for your name;
only the honest can dwell in your presence.

Psalm 141

A PSALM, BY DAVID.

God, I call to you in desperation,
rush to my help.

Let your ears hear my cry
whenever I long for your presence.

Let my prayer come before you
like sweet-smelling incense,

my upraised hands be
like evening sacrifice upon the altar.

Place, God, a watch over my mouth,
a guard at the doorway to my lips.

Don't bend my heart to the temptation of hate,
the urge to treat cruelly toward those
who act with cruelty toward others.

People who spread sorrow—
don't let me partake of their delicacies
or eat from their bread.

Let the righteous rebuke me with kindness,
reprove me for the sake of my soul.

Don't pour anointing oil on my head;
my prayer is still consumed with their wrongs.

Their judges have fallen off cliffs—
if only they would listen to my words,
for I am well intentioned.

Like trees cleaved and ruptured upon the earth,
our bones have been scattered at the mouth of the grave.

For my eyes are toward you, my Hope, my Upholder.
In you I have taken refuge;
don't strip away my life.

Protect me from the teeth of their trap;
save me from the snare of those
who strive to bring harm.

The wrongful will fall into their own nets—
but I will remain unbroken,
passing safely over harm.

Psalm 142

A SONG FOR UNDERSTANDING,
BY DAVID, WHEN HE WAS IN THE CAVE, A PRAYER.

My voice to you cries out for help;
my voice to you pleads for compassion.

I pour out before you
the lake of my complaint.

I have confided to you my constriction
when my spirit grows weak within.

You—you know my path;
on this road that I wander
lurk many pitfalls of ruin.

Look to the right and see
there is for me no fellow traveler;

escape flies from my feet;
no one asks after my soul.

I have cried to you, God, in anguish.
I have said, "You are my refuge,
my portion in the land of the living."

Listen to my bitter cry, for I am brought very low.

Lift me up from all that pursues me,
for my enemies are stronger than I.

Bring my soul from its dark enclosure
to give thanks to your holy name.

With me all the righteous wait to see
whether you will heap blessings in recompense
    upon me.

Psalm 143

>+◦+-◦-◦+◄

A PSALM, BY DAVID.

God, hear the pleading of my prayer.
Open your ears to my cry for compassion.

Answer me with your steadfast presence,
with the clarity of your justice.

Do not judge your servant too harshly,
for compared to your holiness, no creature is just.

A great obstacle pursued my soul;
it ground my life to the dirt.

It made me sit in dark regions,
like those long since dead.

My breath constricted around me;
my heart became like rubble inside.

I remember earlier days,
times I devoted all my waking hours
to pondering your works;

I spoke about the craft of your hands
to all who would listen.

I spread my hands toward you,
my soul like thirsty earth—Selah.

Answer me quickly, God,
my breath wheezes ragged in my chest.

If you hide your face from me,
I will be like those who drown in the pit of death.

Let me hear your kindness each morning
because it is you I have trusted.

Let me know which road's shoulder
I should cling to,
because to you I raise up my soul.

Lift me away from my troubles, God,
for I have concealed them from you until today.

Teach me to do your will,
for you are my God.

With your enlivening spirit
lead me to level ground;
for the sake of your name, Holy One, restore me
    to life.

In your love for humanity,
pull my soul from anguish.
In your kindness, crush my obstacles to dust.

All my torments will dissolve into nothing—
for all my work is for you.

Psalm 144

By David.

Praised is God, my Rock.

The one who teaches my hands to struggle,
my fingers to defend myself during war.

My source of kindness and refuge from pursuit.
My place far from violence, my escape from strife.

My Shield—in my Creator I have found comfort,
the one who brings peace to people under my sway.

God, what are we that you should know us,
mortals that you should consider us so closely?

We are only vapor,
our days like passing shade.

Holy One, bend your heavens and come down;
touch the mountains until they smoke.

Loud flashes of lighting—shatter them.
Send forth your arrows, making them crash in a frenzy,

send forth your hands from the heavens
and shatter me an opening now,

save me from tumultuous water,
undignified death at the hands of a stranger,

those whose mouths speak vanity,
whose right hand is a source of false help.

God, I will sing you a new song,
on the ten-stringed harp I will play melodies.

You who bring salvation to kings,
who helped David, your servant,
escape the bloodthirsty sword,

shatter me an opening now,
save me from undignified death
at the hands of a stranger,

those whose mouths speak vanity,
whose right hand is a source of false help.

For our sons are like saplings,
cultivated with care from their youth,

our daughters are like columns,
their bodies a palace.

Our granaries are full,
overflowing from one kind to another.

Our flocks multiply by the thousands
in the broad fields where they graze.

Our cattle bear their burdens gladly;
there is no break in the fences,
not one escapes.

No shouting erupts in the streets.

Glad is the nation for whom such is their life.
Happy are the people for whom this is their God.

Psalm 145

I will hold you above everything else that exists—
my God, my Holy Protector,

awed by your name always,
in gladness as well as sorrow.

Every day I will bless you,
praising your name repeatedly,
as long as reach of time.

Your signature is everywhere,
praised beyond measure;
your vastness is wide beyond sight.

Generation to generation applauds your acts.
And your unflinching strength—
they continually speak of it.

Majestic is the glory of your splendor;
I will forever speak of your wonders.

Your powerful acts are known by everyone;
your infinite presence I will try to recount.

The world overflows with memory of your goodness—
your righteousness makes all creation cry out in praise.

You are kind and compassionate,
long to anger, endless in love.

Your goodness is everywhere;
your compassion extends to all of your works.

All your creation, God, thanks you;
all the faithful cry out praise of your blessings.

They proclaim the glory of your guidance;
your unflinching strength—they constantly speak of it—

to make known to humanity your strength,
the glory of your eternal presence.

You care for the entire world.
Your governance continues from one generation to the
      next.

You support all who are falling
and straighten those who are bent.

All eyes search for you with hope
and you give them food in its time.

You open up your hand, satisfying
the desires of all life.

You are righteous in all your words,
kind in every act,

close to all who call out,
to all who earnestly call out your name.

The will of those who revere you,
you gladly fulfill.
Hearing their cry, you rush to respond.

You keep watch over those who love you;
names of the wrongful in the end disappear.

My mouth will speak your praises
until all flesh exalts the Holy Name—
and the blessing never stops.

Psalm 146

⊱──◦──⊰

Praise God!

Let my soul stand in wonder of the Holy.
Let my life stand in praise of God.

I will make melodies to my Witness
with the whole of my strength.

Don't put your trust in the wealthy,
mortals who cannot give salvation.

Their breath leaves; they return to their plot of earth.
On that day all their aspirations are lost.

Happy is the one for whom Jacob's Protector is their
    help.
who looks hopefully toward the Holy One, God—

the maker of heaven and earth,
the sea and all that is in it;

who stands faithful with us forever,
who brings justice to the oppressed,

food to the hungry, release for the bound,
who opens the eyes of the blind—

who straightens those hunched over
by sorrow.

God loves the righteous,
keeping watch over strangers,
encouraging orphans and widows.

But the road of the wrongful is twisted.

The Holy One will sustain us forever—
your God, O Zion, from one generation to the next.

Praise God!

Psalm 147

>-+◊>-○-<◊+-<

Halleluyah!
Shine forth your praises to God!

How good it is to sing out to the Creator—

because among the world's pleasures,
praise is most beautiful of all.

You are the one who restores Jerusalem,
gathering the outcast of Israel,

healing the shattered of heart,
and patiently binding their grief.

You number all the stars and give each one a name.
You are infinite, your reach beyond measure.

For the limit of your understanding, there is no count.
You hold up the humble and flatten despisers to the
     ground.

Respond to the Holy with thanksgiving;
sing out to the Creator with your harp—

the one who covers the sky with clouds,
who prepares the ground with rain.

You cause grass to sprout up on the hills,
giving food to the cattle,
young ravens that for which they call.

Not in the loins of horses do you delight;
not in thigh of man do you take pleasure.

You are delighted by those who revere you,
those who wait for your kindness with hope.

Praise, O Jerusalem, your Creator.
Shine forth praises to your Maker, O Zion.

Because God strengthens the bolts of your gates
and blesses your children within—

bringing peace to your borders,
satisfying you with the richest wheat.

The Eternal sends word to the earth;
quickly it runs to become act—

you give snow thick as wool,
scattering a cover of hoarfrost like dust.

You hurl down crystals of ice like bread crumbs—
faced by divine coldness, who can stand?

You speak a word, and ice melts;
you breathe your wind, and water flows forth.

You announce your will to Jacob,
your statutes and judgments to Israel.

Do you do this for every nation?
Do they all have insight of your ways?

Shine forth your praises to God!
Halleluyah!

Psalm 148

>+◦+◦+◦+◦+<

Praise God!

Praise the Creator from the sky,
praise the Eternal from the heights,
let all the angels sing out in praise!

Let the heavenly array praise our Upholder,
the sun and moon praise the Holy Name:
let all bright stars give forth praise.

Praise God, great dome of the sky,
along with the water above even that.
Praise the name of God.

For the Infinite commanded you into being
and you were created.
The Holy One sustains you for all time,
promising a decree that will never end.

Praise the Creator from the earth,
sea serpents and creatures of the deep.
Fire and hail, snow and thunderclouds, wind and
    storm—
each acts in keeping with the holy word.

The mountains and all the hills,
fruit trees and all the cedars,
beasts and cattle,
crawling insects and soaring birds,

kings of the earth and all the nations,
princes and every judge on the earth.
Young men and virgins, old people and youth—
praise the name of God!

For your name alone is exalted.
Your glory is spread over earth and sky.

You lift up a ray of strength for your people,
bringing out praise from all who love you,
from the children of Israel with whom you are close.

Praise God!

Psalm 149

Praise God!
Sing out to God a new song,
praise the Holy One wherever the faithful gather.

Let Israel rejoice in its Maker,
the children of Zion exult in their Source of Hope.

Praise God's name with dancing;
make melodies with the drums and the harp.

For you take pleasure in your people,
beautifying the humble with salvation.

The faithful exult in your glory.

They will sing out upon their beds,
songs of elevation in their throats,
and a double-edged sword in their hands—

to right the wrongs of nations,
to bring rebuke upon countries that rebel,

to imprison their kings with chains,
their tyrants with fetters of iron,

to bring them to you for justice,
as it is written,

your splendor is known to all who love you—
praise God!

Psalm 150

Praise God!
Praise God in holy places,

praise God in the firmament
where heavenly power resides.

Praise God for steadfastness of might,
praise God for greatness beyond measure.

Praise God with a blast of the shofar,
praise God with the harp and the lyre.

Praise God with timbrel and dance,
praise God with the strings and the flute.

Praise God with cymbals that ring loudly,
praise God with cymbals that come crashing down.

Let everything that breathes praise God.
Shine forth your praises on God!

Selected Glossary

An extensive explanation of my translating decisions is available online at www.thecompletepsalms.com. Below is an explanation of the rendering of words of importance that occur with frequency.

Awe of God/*Yirah*: Often translated by others as "fear," and in one of its most common conjugations as "fear of God." But the word can also mean "wonder" or "reverence," a meaning that is more in keeping with the feeling toward God evoked by the psalms. The word is also used in noun forms to describe those who stand in wonder of God. The sense of awe is much like the idea of the sublime, or Rudolf Otto's idea of the "numinous."

Constriction/*Tzar*/*Tzorer*/*Mitzraim*: The root means "constriction" or "narrowness." From this same root we get the word *mitzrayim*, or "Egypt." The flight from Egypt, then, can be read as a flight from places of fear and constriction, and I have sometimes translated the word (as it appears in its many forms) to reflect that. *Tzorer* means "enemy," but as with other words that mean "enemy," I have often chosen to translate it differently. In this case, I frequently translate the word to reflect the inner constriction that comes from outward fear.

Faithful/Loyal/Righteous/*Tzedek*/*Tzadikim*: Translated in most places as "righteous" or "just," the root, which has both noun and adjectival forms, can also suggest loyalty or faithfulness to God's teachings.

Kindness/*Chesed*/*Chasadim*: The word for which the King James Version famously used the term "loving-kindness." Its root means "kindness," not so much as a character attribute as an active principle, kindness in action. It suggests a kind of unchanging, unconditional love. I have rendered it in various ways, sometimes to suggest faithfulness, other times to suggest eternal love.

Leader/Ruler/Melech: Because of my resolution to translate God in a way that is neither masculine nor feminine, I have avoided translating this word as "king," its literal meaning, when referring to God. Instead, I've questioned what the word "kingship" means to evoke in a particular psalm. Some of the qualities involve protection, source of sustenance, holiness, and glory. I draw upon these attributes in my rendering. When it came to human kings, however, I often let the word stand. Sometimes I have used the word "leaders" or "rulers" in its stead, as part of an attempt to make the psalms speak more directly to political issues today.

Missing the mark/twisting away/rebellion/*Chet, avon, pesha*: These Hebrew words, often translated as "sin," each have particular meanings. The word *chet* has to do with missing the mark, as in archery, a sense very different from the word "sin" in English. *Avon* has a sense of having twisted away from the path, and *pesha* suggests a kind of willful rebellion. I have by and large avoided the word "sin," as it is caught up in ideologies of guilt, demonization, and punishment—compared to "missing the mark," for instance, which is an ordinary aspect of existence.

Praised are you/ *Baruch ata*: Almost always translated in other translations as "blessed," but such a word is of ambiguous meaning when it comes to God. What can it mean to say that the Source of Blessing is blessed? The root of the word also means "knee," and so the original sense seems to have been something like "the one to whom we bend our knee in awe." I have used various strategies in an attempt to evoke such an attitude of reverence and wonder.

Salvation/ *Yeshua*: The translation of the Hebrew *yeshua* as "salvation" has a history of controversy. Jews have often balked at the word "salvation," seeing it as too laden with Christian overtones and too heavily associated with Jesus. Some have claimed that the Jewish idea of *yeshua* necessitates human participation and does not simply rely upon divine intervention. But I see no reason that the word "salvation" should be conceded to Christianity and seen as incompatible with Judaism. The word has a grace that other similar words lack, and I have not hesitated to use it. I have also translated it otherwise as seems appropriate, including using, for instance, the word "help." In this, I have tried to be guided by the psalm rather than by territorial concerns between Judaism and Christianity.

Teaching/ *Torah*: The word in Hebrew means both the literal biblical text and, more generally, teaching. I have often translated it as "teaching" and sometimes as "wisdom." For Jews, Torah is the language through which God becomes apparent in the world, and it is in this sense that the word "teaching" should be understood.

To the Conductor of the Eternal Symphony/*L'mantzeach*: Often part of the opening address of a psalm, and usually translated elsewhere as "to the Conductor" or "to the Director." The word's root means both "eternality" and "musical conductor," and in combining these meanings, my intent is to suggest an image of God as the arranger of the many diffuse aspects of existence. While "symphony" is obviously a word that comes from a much later era than the psalms, it suggests an image of what I wanted to convey: a deeply concerned, involved, and orchestrating God.

To the World/Forever/*L'olam*: Means "eternity in both space and time." The recurring refrain in Psalm 136 is, as far as I know, universally translated by others in a temporal sense: "for his kindness lasts forever." Given the psalm's context of divine generosity toward creation, I have translated the line as "For God's kindness is toward the world." I have done similarly on other occasions when relation to the world rather than eternity is the theme.

Wrongful/Fear/*Oyev*/*Rasha*: *Oyev* is usually rendered as "enemy" and *rasha* as "evil one" or "wicked one." I often sidestep the word "enemy" in English, just as I avoid the word "evil," because they suggest polarized and unchangeable states of being. This idea seems to me both spiritually dangerous and biblically inaccurate. Because good and evil are tendencies that can be found in us all, in this translation I try to choose words that emphasize the wrongfulness of a person's behavior, not the irredeemableness of his or her being. As mentioned in the introduction, I also occasionally understand "enemy" to refer to an internal obstacle, not an external threat.

A Note on the Author

Pamela Greenberg is a poet and writer. She has an M.F.A. from Syracuse University and a master's in Jewish studies from Hebrew College, where she received the award in Hebrew literature. She spent a year in rabbinical school before deciding to dedicate herself more fully to writing. She has received several writing awards, including a University Fellows Award at Syracuse and residencies at the Fine Arts Work Center and the Millay Colony for the Arts. An excerpt from her psalms translation appeared in the "Book World" section of the *Washington Post*. She lives in Cambridge, Massachusetts, with her husband and young son.